The Trading
Methodologies
of W.D. Gann

The Trading Methodologies of W.D. Gann

A Guide to Building Your Technical Analysis Toolbox

Hima Reddy

FT PressVice President, Publisher: Tim Moore
Associate Publisher and Director of Marketing: Amy Neidlinger
Executive Editor: Jim Boyd
Editorial Assistant: Pamela Boland
Operations Specialist: Jodi Kemper
Marketing Manager: Megan Graue
Cover Designer: Alan Clements
Managing Editor: Kristy Hart
Senior Project Editor: Lori Lyons
Copy Editor: Krista Hansing Editorial Services
Proofreader: Kathy Ruiz
Indexer: Larry Sweazy
Compositor: Nonie Ratcliff
Manufacturing Buyer: Dan Uhrig

FT Press offers excellent discounts on this book when ordered in quantity for bulk purchases or special sales. For more information, please contact U.S. Corporate and Government Sales, 1-800-382-3419, corpsales@pearsontechgroup.com. For sales outside the U.S., please contact International Sales at international@pearsoned.com.

Company and product names mentioned herein are the trademarks or registered trademarks of their respective owners.

Charts created using TradeStation. ©TradeStation Technologies, Inc. 2001-2012. All rights reserved. No investment or trading advice, recommendation, or opinions is being given or intended.

Pearson Education LTD.
Pearson Education Australia PTY, Limited.
Pearson Education Singapore, Pte. Ltd.
Pearson Education Asia, Ltd.
Pearson Education Canada, Ltd.
Pearson Educación de Mexico, S.A. de C.V.
Pearson Education—Japan
Pearson Education Malaysia, Pte. Ltd.

Library of Congress Cataloging-in-Publication Data

Reddy, Hima, 1979-
  The trading methodologies of W.D. Gann : a guide to building your technical analysis toolbox / Hima
Reddy.
    p. cm.
  ISBN 978-0 13-273438-7 (hbk. : alk. paper)
  1. Technical analysis (Investment analysis) 2. Speculation. 3. Gann, William D., b. 1878. I. Title.
  HG4529.R43 2013
  332.63'2042--dc23
                    2012028203

For my father,
Pandu R. Tadoori

Contents at a Glance

Foreword. xv

Preface. xvii

Chapter 1   The Work of W.D. Gann 1

Chapter 2   Elements of the Market 9

Chapter 3   Interpreting the Market 27

Chapter 4   Trading the Market. 39

Chapter 5   Application of Gann's Principles 85

Chapter 6   Trade and Capital Management 119

Chapter 7   Bringing It All Together. 139

Chapter 8   Beyond Trading Basics. 155

Appendix A   Gann's 28 Trading Rules 173

Appendix B   Affirmative Versions of Gann's 28 Rules. 177

Appendix C   Gann's Buying and Selling Points 181

Appendix D   Gann's Soybean Chart 185

Appendix E   Google, Inc. (GOOG) Highs and Lows by
             Calendar Month 187

Index 189

Contents

Foreword. xv

Preface. xvii

Chapter 1   The Work of W.D. Gann 1
                 Market Predictions. 1
                 Publications 3
                 Focus of This Book 5
                 Trading Rules. 6

Chapter 2   Elements of the Market 9
                 Basic Market Movement 9
                 Price Is King. 10
                 Patterns Repeat 11
                 The Construct of Time 20

Chapter 3   Interpreting the Market. 27
                 Gann's View of Price Movement. 27
                 Projections Based on Existing Price Movement. 32

Chapter 4   Trading the Market. 39
                 Exceeding Moves in Time. 41
                 Triple Bottoms/Tops 49
                 Double Bottoms/Tops 57
                 Exceeding Moves in Price 63
                 Buy Old Tops/Sell Old Bottoms 69
                 Rapid Moves. 74
                 Trading Ranges 80

Chapter 5   Application of Gann's Principles .85
                 Gann's Favorite Numbers 85
                 Gann's Principles Applied Outside of Price 95
                 The Importance of the Closing Price 108

Chapter 6   **Trade and Capital Management** 119

Risk Assessment.....................................120

Placement of Orders 123

Trade Initiation 126

Management of Trade...............................127

Trade Exit...135

Review 136

Chapter 7   **Bringing It All Together**..........................139

Exploring Gann's Examples.........................139

Rigid Rules, Flexible Observation...................150

Chapter 8   **Beyond Trading Basics**...........................155

Looking to the Left of the Chart....................155

Recommended Reading 160

Obtaining Charts 161

Gann's Writing Style and References.................162

A Study "Partner"—an Invaluable Tool 167

The End...of the Beginning.........................170

Appendix A   Gann's 28 Trading Rules 173

Appendix B   Affirmative Versions of Gann's 28 Rules..............177

Appendix C   Gann's Buying and Selling Points 181

Appendix D   Gann's Soybean Chart 185

Appendix E   Google, Inc. (GOOG) Highs and Lows
by Calendar Month..............................187

Index 189

Acknowledgments

Clare White—You introduced me to the opportunity to write this book. I am so thankful for your continued confidence in my skills and knowledge and your thoughtful advice through the changing phases of my career. You are a mentor in the truest sense.

Ken Gerber—You shared your extensive Gann expertise, which added immeasurably to the quality of this book. I greatly appreciate the time and effort you took to answer my questions, critique my ideas, and make suggestions that only a remarkable teacher could.

Nikki Jones—You so graciously wrote the foreword for this book and allowed access to your company's vast Gann resources for my research. I am so grateful for the words of support and encouragement that you provided along the way and for the connection that we have maintained since our first Gann seminar together.

Marnie Owen—You provided impressively detailed and thoughtful reviews of my book material as it developed from a rough draft to a complete manuscript. I am extremely thankful for you in my life, as a dear friend and as a knowledgeable colleague with whom I can share my fascination with technical analysis and the markets.

Jim Boyd—As my publisher, you took a chance on me. I am so grateful for all the guidance and insight you provided through the writing and production processes.

Kristy Hart, Lori Lyons, Krista Hansing, and the rest of the Pearson production team—You transformed my book from a manuscript draft to a press-ready work! Thank you for your helpful suggestions and painstaking efforts, which improved the layout of the book while maintaining its context and intent.

All of my extended family, friends, and colleagues—You express enthusiasm in my work and exude a perpetual interest in reading what I create, whether it's been a blog post, or this book! I am very thankful for you, and I am inspired by each and every one of you.

Mom, Dad, Rekha, Swathi, and Abhi—Your patience, love, and support are invaluable. Thank you for motivating me to try and be the best at what I do. It makes me want to be a better daughter and sister as well.

Srinu—You ground me when my head gets into the clouds, but know when to let me fly free. I am so grateful for your encouragement and support in all of my endeavors. Beginning work on this book in 2011 was the second best thing I did that year. The first was marrying you.

About the Author

Hima Reddy, CMT, was first introduced to technical analysis, and to the works of W.D. Gann, during her high school years by her father, who has had a passion for trading and the markets since the early 1980s. However, it wasn't until after she completed an undergraduate Finance degree at Indiana University's Kelley School of Business, and returned to her home state of New York in 2001, that she immersed herself in the markets. She simultaneously volunteered as a sponsorship coordinator for several Market Technicians Association conferences, traded equity and commodity futures under the tutelage and guidance of her father, and completed the Chartered Market Technician certification. In 2006, she joined Informa Global Markets, an independent financial research firm providing live, 24-hour market analysis. As Senior Technical Analyst, she was responsible for producing timely and accurate short-term technical analysis and trading strategies for fixed income and FX markets. With analysis ranging through multiple timeframes, her team also prepared written updates covering longer-term trends. Hima's "guru" has always been Gann—the first market analysis book she ever studied in-depth was *How to Make Profits in Commodities*—and to this day that is her go-to guide to the markets. Since 2011 she has returned to trading independently and continues to write about the financial markets. Her primary methods of technical analysis include pattern recognition and time duration relationships within markets based on Gann's methodology, momentum assessment through the use of the Relative Strength Index (RSI), Fibonacci relationships, and moving average systems including the use of channels for trade management. Hima now resides with her husband in Baltimore, Maryland.

Foreword

Over the years, many questions have been asked about W.D. Gann and his trading system. Does it work? How much time do I have to spend before I trade? Can I make money? Where do I begin? I believe the best question of all is, "Which one of Gann's books can I read that will teach me how to trade?" The answer is, *they all will.* However, never has a more worthy book exploring Gann's been written for beginners or intermediate traders as this one.

To be a successful trader, you need to know the rules that have stood the test of time, a bit about the man who created them, and about the author who wrote this book.

Hima Reddy has provided us with the "missing link" to W.D. Gann's trading methods. In this book, she has laid out the basic plans step by step, along with examples, which can be easily followed by anyone with an interest in learning the potential profit areas in trading.

Reddy is an extremely talented and determined person. She is well-qualified, with several years working as a professional in the financial world. I first met her at the W.D. Gann Experience Trading Seminar in 2003. I could see that she possessed the knowledge and determination it takes to be a successful market trader.

In the trading world, it seems as if everyone has heard of W.D. Gann, one of the most successful traders and market forecasters of all time. For more than 50 years, the accuracy of his forecasts and his trading successes stunned the commodities and securities world. He became one of the mystic traders of his time, which earned him the title "Guru of Wall Street." A prolific chartist, analyst, and writer, Gann recorded his methods and systems of trading in books and courses that are today among the most well-known and sought-after books on market trading.

The Trading Methodologies of W.D. Gann: A Guide to Building Your Technical Analysis Tool Box is a solid, beginning stepping stone you can count on. This book will open your mind to new ideas that can be extremely valuable to you financially.

Reddy has openly shared her goals and the path you must take to achieve yours. She is more than willing to share with those who are receptive.

Her answers are always words of encouragement: "Keep going."

Nikki Jones
Lambert-Gann Publishing Company

Preface

"Life affords no greater pleasure than that of helping others who are trying to help themselves."

—W. D. Gann[1]

When I was 16 years old, I was doing chemistry homework one night and stopped in my father's office to get some assistance with my assignment. I saw my father studying a graph of some sort displayed on his computer screen. I asked him what he was looking at, and he said it was a chart plotting the changes in a stock price; he was using the chart to help him trade the stock. When I asked how he was doing that, he explained that he was using the mathematical relationships present in the stock's price history to help him determine whether the price of the stock would likely go up or down so that he could buy or sell shares of the stock accordingly.

I was intrigued. (I've always been a "math geek," so that wasn't surprising.) I told my father that I wanted to know more about this type of financial analysis. I asked him about the possibilities of learning more about it in college, and he told me that the subject was not very popular and that I likely would not come across it while at school. However, he did offer to help me learn about trading through books and by following his stock charts. Over the next few months, he gave me his old edition (printed in 1976) of Gann's *How to Make Profits Trading in Commodities*. He told me to read that book over and over and glean Gann's methods from it. Seventeen years later, he gives me

---

[1] W. D. Gann, *How to Make Profits Trading in Commodities* (Pomeroy, WA: Lambert-Gann, 2009), Foreword.

the same advice—keep studying the works of Gann's great mind and incorporate what I learn into my own trading plan.

Back when I was in high school and college, as a young person with no experience with the markets, I had to teach myself the methods presented in Gann's works. I did this by synthesizing the concepts into smaller pieces that I could grasp. With knowledge gained through these smaller tenets, I annotated countless charts both on my computer and by hand. I then synthesized into my own trading plan the buy and sell signals and trade management concepts that I understood and witnessed, and I continued to collect examples of charts that illustrated the relating theories. I even began to create market newsletters for myself, focusing on one security at a time and looking at its key price points. This was all to help me better understand Gann's main points and methods so that I could profitably apply them to my trading.

I eventually obtained my Chartered Market Technician (CMT) designation, administered by the Market Technicians Association (www.mta.org). I then worked as a professional technical analyst for several years. However, what I learned from Gann's teachings has remained my prime trading guide.

The chapters ahead contain my humble attempt to present my self-taught interpretation of some of Gann's major works. His writings are among the most esoterically written trading and investing materials out there. However, over the course of my study, I have been able to make them my own. Hopefully, the research I've done into Gann's trading methodology will enable you to grasp the concepts quickly and incorporate them immediately into your own investing/trading.

Anyone who has looked at Gann's works sees that he used many chart examples to illustrate his trading rules and philosophies. I do the same, and I expand the realm to include securities that many of us observe regularly. I apply the trading rules and ideas to modern charts. You'll likely see that, among the charts I use, many of them are drawn from market observations made *after* I began conducting research for this book (December 2010).

I hope you, the reader, find that this helps you improve your own trading toolkit. My goal is not to make you a Gann expert through this book alone: I believe that trading education is an ongoing process and can't come from any one person or resource. I do, however, hope that I am speaking to the part of you that is akin to the 16-year-old I once was—eager to venture into a deeper study of Gann's materials for the most complete approach to this master's investing methodologies.

1

The Work of W.D. Gann

Market Predictions

As an author, I want to give you a reason to read this book that goes beyond my assurances that the material is useful. So I want to begin by referring you to some of Gann's greatest market predictions and how he profited from those moves. Throughout Gann's works, he advised his students to use all their trading and forecasting tools all the time to discover the forces at work in any given market. Therefore, sharing his forecasting/trading successes should give you confidence that the information ahead in this book will help improve your own investing methods.

One of the most concise and publicly accessible records of Gann's market predictions is an article written by Richard D. Wyckoff in December 1909, titled "William D. Gann: An Operator Whose Science and Ability Place Him in the Front Rank—His Remarkable Predictions and Trading Record." The article was published in Volume 5 (Number 2) of the *Ticker and Investment Digest*, a very influential stock market publication at the time.

The first part of the article directly explores Gann's general methods of market analysis. Later in the article, Wyckoff shares the findings of William E. Gilley, who was brought in to validate the success (or failure) of Gann's methods. Gilley was an Inspector of Imports in New York with 25 years of experience with the markets. During the time that Gilley observed Gann, he watched Gann make 286 trades. Of those, 264 were winning trades, for a success rate of 92 percent![1]

Above all, Gilley documented a series of predictions that Gann made during October 1909. Some of Gann's more remarkable predictions are as follows:

Union Pacific (stock)

"In 1908 when Union Pacific was 168 1/8, he told me that it would not touch 169 before it had a good break. We sold it short all the way down to 152 3/8, covering on the weak spots and putting it out again on the rallies, securing a 23 points profit out of an eighteen-point move."

United States Steel (stock)

"He came to me when United States Steel was selling around 50 and said 'This Steel will run up from 58 but it will not sell at 59. From there it should break 16 3/4 points.' We sold it short around 58 3/8 with a stop at 59. The highest it went was 58 3/4. From there it declined to 41 1/4 – 17 1/2 points."

Wheat (commodity futures)

"At another time wheat was selling at about 89¢. He predicted that the May option would sell at $1.35. We bought it and made large profits on the way up. It actually touched $1.35 1/2."

Wheat

"One of the most astonishing calculations made by Mr. Gann was during last summer (1909) when he predicted that September wheat would sell at $1.20. This meant that it must touch that figure before the end of the month of September. At twelve o'clock, Chicago time, on September 30th (the last day) the option was selling below $1.08, and it looked as

---

[1] *The Natural Squares Calculator* course workbook (Pomeroy, WA: Lambert-Gann, 2002), 10–12.

though his prediction would not be fulfilled. Mr. Gann said 'If it does not touch $1.20 by the close of the market it will prove that there is something wrong with my whole method of calculation. I do not care what price it is now, it must go there.' It is common history that September wheat surprised the whole country by selling at $1.20 and no higher in the very last hour of the trading, closing at that figure."

United States Steel

"In our presence Mr. Gann sold Steel common short at 94 7/8, saying that it would not go to 95. It did not.

On a drive which occurred during the week ending October 29th, Mr. Gann bought Steel common at 86 1/4, saying that it would not go to 86. The lowest it sold was 86 1/8."

I hope that Gilley's observations presented within the context of Wyckoff's article have brought your attention to what Gann was able to accomplish investing in the markets. Gann dedicated his life's work to understanding the markets and the principles that govern them, and it is no small feat to have such insight. This is why what Gann had to share through his books and courses is of such great value. The lessons taught in those pages are among the tools he used to master the market as he did.

Publications

W.D. Gann wrote several books. Of these, five open with a portrait of Gann. Every time I see one of those portraits, I feel that his expression conveys the following—"Trading is serious business. Get ready to work hard and come out a more successful trader on the other side." To impart his trading wisdom, Gann published the following titles:

- *Truth of the Stock Tape* (1923)
- *Tunnel Thru the Air* (1927)
- *Wall Street Stock Selector* (1930)
- *New Stock Trend Detector* (1936)
- *How to Make Profits Trading in Puts and Calls* (1937)
- *Face Facts America* (1940)
- *How to Make Profits Trading in Commodities* (1941)
- *45 Years in Wall Street* (1949)
- *Magic Word* (1950)

He also put together market courses. Both his Stock Market Course and his greater Master Commodity Course were ready for purchase by 1950—the Stock Course for $2,500, and the Commodity course for $5,000. According to the U.S. Inflation Calculator (www.usinflationcalculator.com), in today's dollars, those values equate to more than $23,800 and $47,700, respectively!

All these books and courses are available for purchase through the Lambert-Gann Publishing Company (www.wdgann.com). Generally, experts recommend studying Gann's works in the order in which he wrote them. All his books present trading tools and ideas that can be directly applied to the markets. However, I focus primarily on *How to Make Profits Trading in Commodities* because it is the book my father first handed me when introducing me to Gann's works. I asked my father why he chose this particular book, and he said he had come to learn that it clearly delineated rules pertaining to a few important topics. The first was on protecting a position in the market by using stop orders. The second category was "buying points," the terminology Gann used to describe signals to buy into the market, or go long. The third category was "selling points," describing how to sell into the market, or go short. My father said the *Commodities* book not only explored these key topics, but also presented many examples to reinforce the stated rules, making it easier to directly apply the concepts to any market.

In *How to Make Profits Trading in Commodities*, the following always jumped out to me in the Foreword, written by Gann himself: "I do not believe in gambling or reckless speculation, but am firmly convinced, after years of experience, that if traders will follow rules and trade on definite indications, that speculation can be made a profitable profession." Right there we have the keys—follow the rules and trade on definite indications. But what comprises that? The chapters ahead explore those rules and tenets.

Gann also wrote, "Trading in commodities is not a gambling business, as some people think, but a practical, safe business when conducted on business principles." You may be wondering, just what are Gann's "business principles"? You will discover these in the pages ahead.

Focus of This Book

From all the original materials studied by many Gann experts, Gann's work can fall into one of two categories. The first is trading methodologies. How did Gann actually trade the market? He developed a system of rules that he applied in a consistent and disciplined manner. *That* is information that I explore in this book so that you can directly apply it to your charts.

The second category of Gann's work is forecasting methodologies. Gann employed a multitude of forecasting methods, such as measuring angles on his handwritten charts and using natural squares. These were among the prime tools he used to make predictions about future market action. Forecasting tools cover *when* to invest. But trading methodologies cover *how* to invest, returning to the title of this book.

The chapters ahead contain many of Gann's trading principles and methods, interpreted through both diagrams I've created and chart examples. Toward the end of the book, I show you how Gann combined these tools, and I guide you in learning more directly from his written works. I believe that the greatest value in what I've provided lies in the individual examples. They all apply directly to any market you choose to trade, and I encourage you to follow along with the details of each example as it is presented.

Trading Rules

Some of the other books that analyze Gann's works, and many of the websites and blogs that touch upon the subject, explore an important list of trading rules that Gann wrote back in 1949. *45 Years on Wall Street* lists 24 "never-failing" trading rules based upon Gann's personal experience (see p. 16 and 17 there). However, eight years earlier, Gann had published a list of 28 "valuable" rules in *How to Make Profits Trading in Commodities* (see p. 43 there). From the list of 28 rules to the list of 24 rules, Gann altered only a few rules, due to the focus of the subject matter (stocks versus commodities).

Appendix A of this book contains Gann's original 28 rules, incorporating the stock-related edits. As you can see, many of Gann's rules use negative words, such as *never* and *don't,* to get his points across. The last of the 28 rules even states, "Avoid getting in wrong and out wrong; getting in right and out wrong; this is making double mistakes." This rule really resonated with me when I first read it. It made me realize that if I could break down the elements of my thoughts and actions (essentially, these rules), I would be more likely to do the one thing Gann wanted his students to do but that he didn't say outright: Get in (the market) right, and get out right.

To focus on correct action, I decided to go through Gann's rules and rephrase any that were written with negative language. Why? Because I believe that telling students what they *should* or *can* do is a more effective teaching method than telling them what they *shouldn't* or *can't* do.

Therefore, Appendix B includes a second list of Gann's rules, but in their "affirmative" form. I refer to the "affirmative" rules throughout this book where applicable.

To begin...

> **Gann Rule (Affirmative) #26:** Only follow another man's advice if you know that he knows more than you do.

I'm sharing this rule first to encourage you to explore the rest of this book proactively. I have come to see how Gann's trading methodologies work time and time again, but don't take my word for it. Examine the examples and even observe your own markets of interest to see the knowledge at work.

2

Elements of the Market

Basic Market Movement

According to Gann, a trend makes an advance or decline in three to four "sections." Essentially, any bull or bear market run will play out as shown in Figures 2.1 through 2.4.

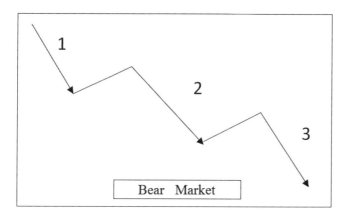

Figure 2.1 Three-section Bear Market

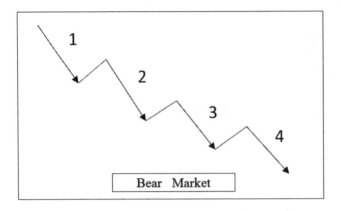

Figure 2.2 Four-section Bear Market

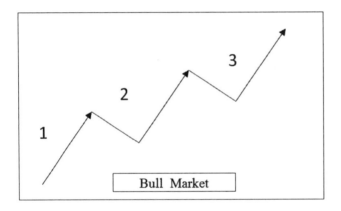

Figure 2.3 Three-section Bull Market

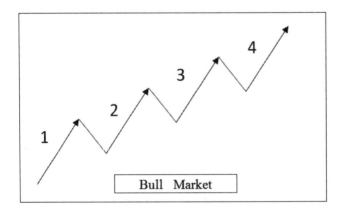

Figure 2.4 Four-section Bull Market

Figures 2.1–2.4 are *not* drawn to scale and are not measuring any amount of price or time movement—they are just showing the *direction* of price movement.

I created these figures to give you clear visual aids in understanding basic market movement. However, it is important to take a moment to note that Gann does not teach using illustrations of concepts. He teaches by using direct examples of live security charts.

Therefore, the security charts that I plot in this book are all OHLC (open high low close) charts, commonly referred to as bar charts. Gann drew his charts by hand, so nearly all of them are drawn in the OHLC style. Therefore, I believe that presenting bar charts is the best way to keep the focus of the chart examples on Gann's methods.

I also plot price bars in a uniform color (black). Those of you who have access to charting software may know that some charting systems plot bars in green when the closing prices are above the opening prices, or red, for when the closing prices are below the opening prices. My software, TradeStation, has similar capacities. But for the purpose of studying the tenets in this book, I think it's best to keep it simple. For that reason, I use black price bars against a white background.

Now we return to the basic tenets of Gann's works.

Price Is King

According to the *Oxford Dictionary* (oxforddictionaries.com), the word *king* may be defined as "a person or thing regarded as the finest or most important in its sphere or group." This is what I'm getting at when I say, "Price is king." When it comes to market analysis, price action is the key determinant of sound, profitable, reliable analysis.

In a true monarchy, the demands of every citizen and the supply of goods and services to meet those demands might shift, but ultimately, the king has the power to decide which dominates. Similarly, the demand and supply within the context of a market will ebb and flow, but the agreed-upon price ultimately determines whether buyers or sellers are in the lead.

Price discounts every factor that you think may be affecting your trading or investing decisions. At first, many people find it hard to believe that big news stories or economic data reports can already be accounted for in the price movement, but it is true. It is true simply because everyone with a vested interest in a particular market is acting on that interest by buying, selling, or waiting on the sidelines. If they are waiting on the sidelines, no matter how rich or powerful or knowledgeable they are, they are not influencing price movement, period. If they are buying or selling, no matter how small a position they take or what they use as basis for their decisions, the action of the buyers and sellers reflects all the factors that could be affecting the security. So when a company announces its earnings, for example, the information itself does not influence the subsequent price movement. The traders' *reactions* to the information are what may cause any erratic price movements.

Examples throughout this book illustrate the importance of focusing on price when analyzing the markets for a trading opportunity.

Patterns Repeat

The definition of the word *pattern,* as explained by Merriam-Webster, is "a form or model proposed for imitation." Within the context of the financial markets, a pattern is a reoccurring series of actions. Why do things reoccur? Why do patterns repeat themselves? One answer for this can be tied to what Gann once wrote: "Everything in existence is based on exact proportion and perfect relation. There is no chance in nature because mathematical principles of the highest order are at the foundation of all things."[1]

Returning to price, although it may seem at times that price is moving randomly within a market, there is always a mathematical relationship in a move to another. To illustrate this on the most basic level, let's examine the possibilities of comparisons between charts.

Looking at two securities that have no direct relationship (such as economic sector), patterns can and do often repeat.

Take a look at Figure 2.5.

From August 1, 2011, to November 25, 2011, NZDUSD (New Zealand dollar priced in terms of the U.S. dollar) declined over the course of three sections. A higher pivot (turn) then formed very close to a key previous low former level. The market then rallied from there.

Now look at Figure 2.6, another chart of a completely different security.

Micron Technology declined from April 27, 2011, to October 4, 2011, over the course of three sections. A higher pivot then formed very close to a key previous low former level. The market rallied from there.

In this comparison, I have combined segments of price movements into relatively large patterns, considering their impact on future price action. In some cases, this is an extension of the traditional technical analysis treatment. This is because I want to drive home the point that any *consistently tradable* market setup can be considered a pattern. They are valid entry and exit signals because they have occurred many times in the past, and the probability of their outcomes is weighted toward specific scenarios. Keep this in mind as you explore Gann's specific buying and selling points in Chapter 4.

---

[1] W.D. Gann, *How to Make Profits Trading in Commodities* (Pomeroy, WA: Lambert-Gann, 2009), p. 34.

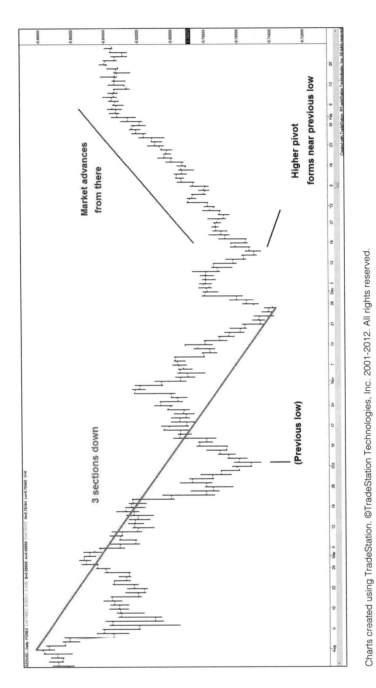

Figure 2.5 NZDUSD, daily, as of March 7, 2012

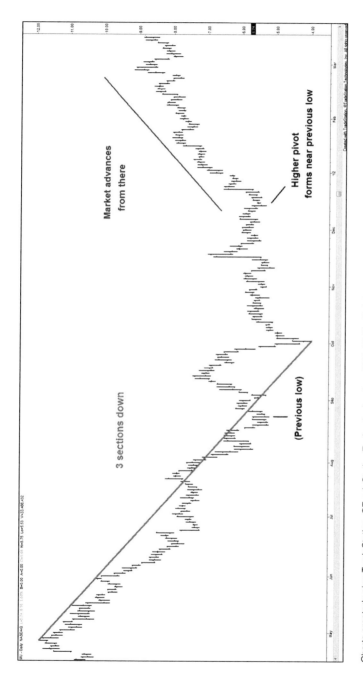

Charts created using TradeStation. ©TradeStation Technologies, Inc. 2001-2012. All rights reserved.

Figure 2.6 MU, daily, as of March 7, 2012

In exploring patterns, we've compared two different securities on one time frame. Now let's look at a single security to see consecutive patterns emerging over one time frame.

Figure 2.7 depicts a daily chart of the September 2012 Wheat futures contract. As you can see, a series of converging trade patterns has been delineated. These patterns are tradable in two ways. The traditional method is to watch for a breakout or breakdown (all three of these patterns happened to exhibit a breakdown). The second method is to watch for trade opportunities using the boundaries themselves as entry and exit points. For example, within the first pattern delineated toward the top of the chart, as the pattern emerged in real time, you could use Gann's buying points to enter long positions from the lower boundary of the formation. You could also use Gann's selling points to enter short positions from the upper boundary of the pattern. The exact buying and selling techniques are explored shortly, but it's important to understand the significance of patterns as they emerge in markets and how they enhance the ability to trade the underlying security.

Lastly, let's look at one security, but over two different time frames to see what patterns emerge within both.

Figure 2.8 shows a weekly chart of Microsoft. Following the decline from $31.58 (April 23, 2010 high) to $22.73 (July 1, 2010 low), a period of sideways trading commenced. The period of trading took on a triangular, converging form, and a breakout did not appear until the week of January 6, 2012.

Figure 2.9 shows a daily chart of Microsoft. After the rally from $23.65 (June 16, 2011 low) to $28.15 (July 26, 2011 high), a period of sideways trading commenced. Interestingly, this triangular, converging trading took place within the context of the price action of Figure 2.8. The breakout of the daily pattern coincided with the breakout of the weekly pattern, occurring in the daily chart on January 4, 2012.

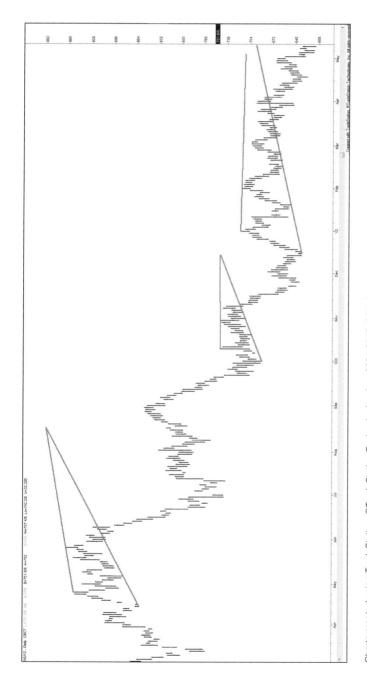

Charts created using TradeStation. ©TradeStation Technologies, Inc. 2001-2012. All rights reserved.

Figure 2.7 WU12, daily, as of May 3, 2012

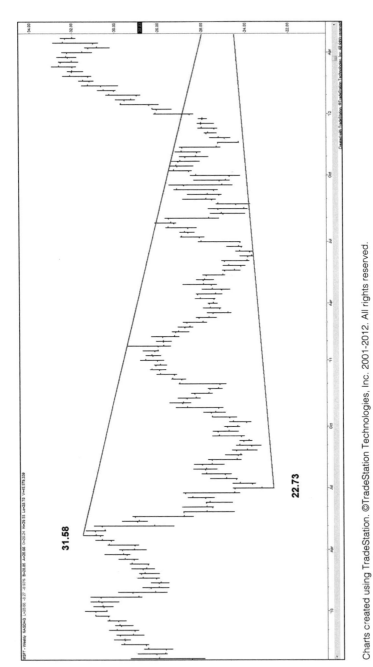

Figure 2.8 MSFT, weekly, as of April 27, 2012

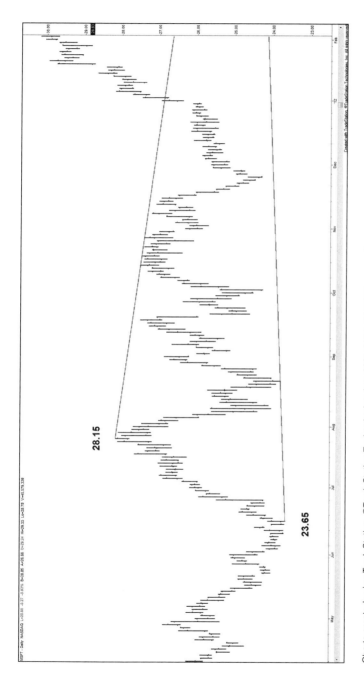

Charts created using TradeStation. ©TradeStation Technologies, Inc. 2001-2012. All rights reserved.

Figure 2.9 MSFT, daily, as of February 2, 2012

The goal of these examples is to introduce the idea that all the action of price and formation of patterns are directly related to mathematical relationships within the markets. This is why similar patterns emerge in different markets and also different time frames. Even though I've focused on triangular patterns for these examples, all types of patterns repeat in markets. The examples throughout this book show that.

The Construct of Time

Gann references days, weeks, months, and years in his books. He specifically says that the more time "between the top and bottom, the more important it is."[2] This means that, the longer a market move endures, whether it's a rally or a decline, the more significant its ending pattern (top or bottom) will be in terms of subsequent price action. However, as I will show in real chart examples of specific buying and selling points, it is evident that these price-and-pattern relationships can play out in any time frame and for any duration of time. For example, a five-minute chart of Soybean futures can illustrate the same pattern that you may see on a quarterly (three months per period) U.S. bond futures chart.

Let's move from time relative to patterns and back to time in relation to price. To ultimately master Gann's most advanced techniques, we must accept the following: Gann talks about price and time in such similar capacity because they are completely related. The source of man's time and the source of man's price system are the same. Here's a thought process to help you follow what I mean by this statement. At its most basic level, time is a system used to measure our location on Earth in relation to other bodies in the universe. At 12:00 a.m. on any January 1, we celebrate the passage of one year of time, but really

---

[2] W.D. Gann, *How to Make Profits Trading in Commodities* (Pomeroy, WA: Lambert-Gann, 2009), p. 42.

we are celebrating the fact that the Earth has completed one full orbit around the Sun. Over the course of any day, we move through our work, play, and rest according to the hands of a clock that we (human beings) invented but that is just our attempt at measuring something that exists whether we measure it or not! The planets do not rotate on axes or move about the sun (and each other) because we measure time. Instead, man has developed the system of time to account for such movements through space. If you've ever looked at a calendar or clock and utilized what you saw to make decisions in your life, then you have directly related your life's actions to the movements of the planet you inhabit and the celestial bodies that surround it.

Now let's think about price. Again, it is a "man-made" measurement of the value of some entity. Relative to our study, it is the measurement of the value of an object (a stock share, a futures contract, and so on). This value is derived from the supply and demand for the object. Supply and demand are based in human wants and needs, and these rise and decline in direct relation to human psychology and emotions.

All prices are reflections of the complete value that humans give to objects. Because all humans operate within the created context of time, price is directly linked to time.

This is a difficult thing for most beginning traders/investors to grasp because our culture has taught us that *man* creates. In reality, we don't create anything new—we only re-create and re-present things that have already been presented to us and/or are at our disposal. As you continue your exploration of Gann's works, what I'm saying will make more and more sense.

So accepting that price and time are essentially the same, if "price is king," time rules right by its side. The two axes of any security chart involve price and time, and as long as you study these two measurements, you can use Gann's methodologies to make more accurate and successful trades and investments.

Once again, time has now been revealed as a construct of sorts. Therefore, it may not be so difficult for you to understand that, no matter what chart time frame is used to plot a security's price data, the effectiveness of price-based trading methodologies will not change.

Figure 2.10 examines a weekly chart of Google. The company's initial public offering took place on August 19, 2004. The uptrend off the low placed that day at $95.96 and extended for more than three years, reaching a high of $747.24 (November 7, 2007) before a severe downturn.

Figure 2.11 looks at the daily price action of the same stock. The chart shows that price movement similar to the movement in Figure 2.10 occurred off the new major low that was posted at $247.30 (November 21, 2008).

Moving on to the intraday level, Figure 2.12 presents an instance in which the same type of price action showed itself on the 60-minute chart.

What does this demonstrate? The rules of price action are the same *no matter* what time frame you are observing. The same price movements that occur on a weekly chart of a security can occur on another time frame of that same security. The point/dollar range of the moves is likely to differ between time frames because, the larger the time frame, the more data is captured. For example, a month's worth of price data is generally expected to create a greater price range than a day's worth of price data. However, the structures of the price action will be the same. As you observe multiple securities over time, you will see how often similar price developments continue to present themselves within the same security over multiple time frames.

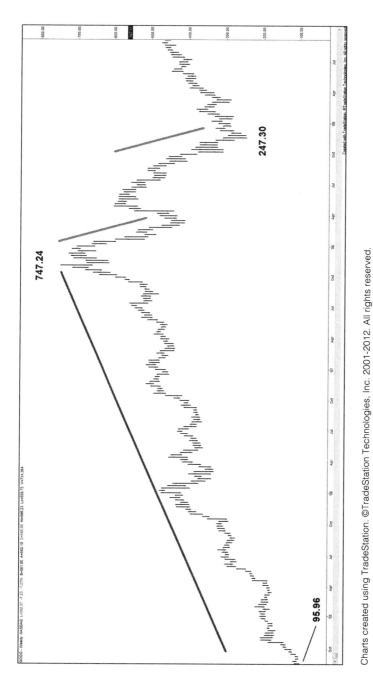

Figure 2.10 GOOG, weekly, as of September 4, 2009

Charts created using TradeStation. ©TradeStation Technologies, Inc. 2001-2012. All rights reserved.

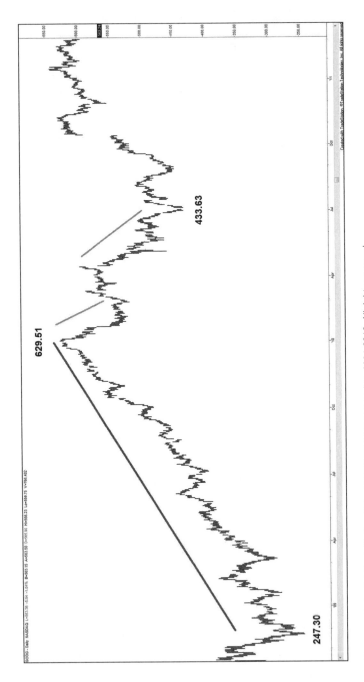

Figure 2.11 GOOG, daily, as of March 3, 2011

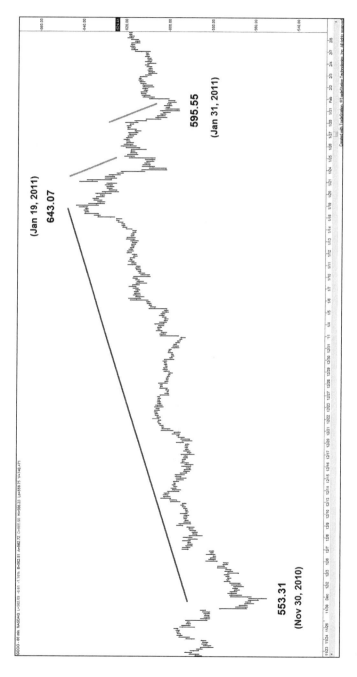

Charts created using TradeStation. ©TradeStation Technologies, Inc. 2001-2012. All rights reserved.

Figure 2.12 GOOG, 60 minutes, as of February 8, 2011

Some of what I shared relating to price, patterns, and time may seem redundant. That's because these three elements connect on many different levels. The only way to absorb these relationships is to study examples over and over again. Take these ideas to your own market observation, and keep track of the relationships you uncover. They will strengthen your understanding of how the basic elements of the market move together to create one seamless representation of a security's activity.

3

Interpreting the Market

Gann's View of Price Movement

This chapter begins with an exercise to connect you with Gann's most fundamental views on how price fluctuates. It may be a bit rudimentary for a seasoned analyst, but it never hurts to take a fresh look at something one has been familiar with for so long. For the reader new to price charts and Gann's works, this is an excellent way to get started.

Procure a blank sheet of paper and a pencil for the following exercise. First, draw a horizontal line just above the bottom of the paper, all the way across. Next, draw a vertical line just inside the right edge of the paper. Your sheet of paper should look like Figure 3.1.

Figure 3.1 Drawing exercise template

Now picture a stock chart. Close your eyes to gather the details of the image you see for a few moments. Then open your eyes. Roughly sketch on paper the image that you had in your mind's eye, remaining above the horizontal line and to the left of the vertical line that you already sketched.

What does your stock chart image look like? One possibility is jagged lines with high points and low points. Another is a gentle curve. It could be a steadily rising line with minor high points and low points along the way. Most people envision price charts with smaller segments that connect within a bigger picture. However, if you pictured and drew a relatively straight line, that's fine, too.

Bring your attention back to your drawing, and focus on the first data point on your chart. This is most likely the first mark you drew toward the left side of your paper. It represents the first point marking a traded price, relating to the vertical line (representing the price axis), and a particular time, relating to the horizontal line (representing the time axis). Label this point as A.

Move your eyes toward the right side of the paper. If point A is lower than the points that follow it, move toward the right to find the immediate next high point, and label that high point as B. If point A marks a high, find the immediate next low that appears after it, and label that B. If the data points in your drawing are clustered close together, just jump ahead to find a second point. All that matters is that the second point you move to be at the end of a move (or section), whether higher or lower, off the first point. You should have only two points marked: A and B.

Looking at the path from point A to point B, what would you say is the most significant location between the two? Let's move to a real-life analogy to help zero in on the answer.

Imagine that you are a pilot commanding a plane that intends to travel from New York to London. You would obviously have to be aware of the distance to be covered on the journey, the amount of fuel required to complete it, and whether your aircraft has that amount of fuel. Another point to be aware of is the radius of action. According to the *Oxford English Dictionary*, the radius of action is a technical term in air navigation used to refer to the point on a flight at which, due to fuel consumption, a plane is no longer capable of returning to the airfield from which it originated. Given the path from New York (point A) to London (point B), what would be the radius of action? Presuming that the fuel levels had been adjusted to be able to cover this journey precisely, the radius of action would be the halfway point of the distance from New York to London. If your plane were to come up to the halfway point of the journey, it would still have enough fuel reserved to turn around and return to New York successfully. However, if the plane passed the halfway point, the remaining amount of fuel would be less than what was used to cover the initial leg of the journey, so the plane would *not* be able to turn around and return to New York.

So back to the path on the stock chart from point A to point B, what is the most significant location between the two? You may answer, "I don't know." You may think there are an infinite number of points from which to choose. Or, still following the analogy to the radius of action, you may say, "The halfway point!" Returning to the line segment as part of a stock chart, the market may *rest* if the halfway point between A and B is not surpassed, and may return toward A before (if) any second attempt toward B is made. As described here, in geometry terms, the midpoint (middle point) equally divides a line segment into two equal parts. In fraction terms, it is the 1/2 point. In percentage terms, it is 50%.

Using percentage terms, let's revisit points A and B. Let's give the A anchor point a value of 0 and the B anchor point a value of 100 so that the 50% level equals 50 in value as well as percentage terms. Draw a dashed horizontal line through A (0) and another horizontal line (which will be parallel) to B (100). Draw a dashed horizontal line through the 50% level between these two points. You now have a segment of space located between the 0 line and the 50% line, and another segment of space between the 50% line and the 100 line.

Looking at these two new segments of space created by finding the 50% level between A and B, you can divide each space once again. The midpoint of 0 to 50 is 25. Draw a horizontal line equidistant from the 0 line and the 50% line, to represent 25%. The midpoint of 50 to 100 is 75. Draw a horizontal line equidistant from the 50% line and the 100 line, to represent 75%. Now there are three special markers on the road from A to B; 25, 50, and 75.

Now divide one last time. The midpoint of 0 to 25 is 12.5. Draw a horizontal line equidistant from the 0 line and the 25% line to represent 12.5%. The midpoint of 25 to 50 is 37.5. Draw a horizontal line equidistant from the 25% line and the 50% line to represent 37.5%. The midpoint of 50 to 75 is 62.5. Draw a horizontal line equidistant from the 50% line and 75% line to represent 62.5%. Lastly, the midpoint of 75 to 100 is 87.5. Draw a horizontal line equidistant from the 75% line and the 100% line to represent 87.5%.

Your paper should now look like Figure 3.2.

Congratulations! You've just uncovered eighths retracement levels. Gann was the first to write about using eighths retracements for market analysis and trading. A retracement in a market is a correction within the context of the greater trend. In an uptrend, a retracement is a corrective move lower before high prices are seen. In a downtrend, a retracement is a corrective move higher before lower prices are seen. The percentage levels created when breaking down a move into eighths are 0, 12.5, 25, 37.5, 50, 62.5, 75, 87.5, and 100. You can also measure retracements as fractions (0, 1/8, 2/8, 3/8, and so on). Either way, these retracement levels are all key areas to watch for a resumption of the existing trend when a retracement is in place, or for the beginning of a change of trend. The 50% level of any move is the most significant area to consider as a potential turning point of the price action. A change in price direction would be likely if the market ever approaches, precisely touches, or probes and bounces from that level. Respecting the 50% level on a dip down within a steadily rising market will create a price floor, or "support." Respecting the 50% level on a rally within a steadily falling market creates a price ceiling, or "resistance."

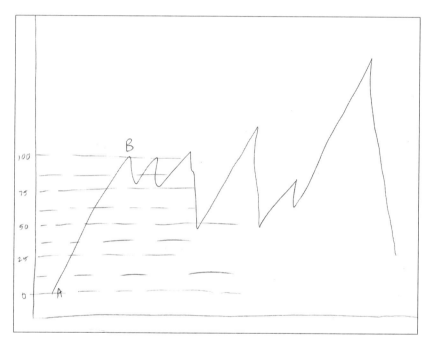

Figure 3.2 Completed drawing exercise

Figure 3.3 illustrates eighths retracements. The support and resistance levels are derived from a particular segment of market action. During the drawing exercise, you looked closely at a move from a price point A to a price point B, but the subsequent moves to a point C, a point D, and onwards would provide the other derivations of support and resistance, as shown in Figure 3.4.

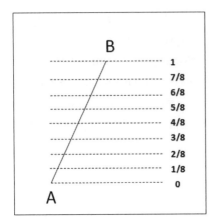

Figure 3.3 AB eighths retracements

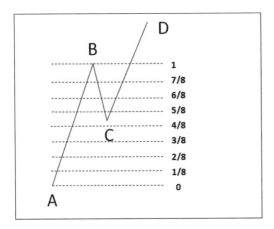

Figure 3.4 AB eighths retracements showing ABCD

Projections Based on Existing Price Movement

Referring back to the statement that every move is mathematically related to another, as you can plainly see on any security chart, many different moves make up the flow of a market. For example, a section higher in an uptrend on a weekly chart can be viewed in smaller segments on a daily chart, consisting of sections higher as well as corrections lower. The moves themselves may occur within a clear uptrend, clear downtrend, or nontrending situation. So, how can you ultimately determine what move or moves to use to project future price action?

Remember back to the AB segment noted on your sketch of stock market action. If AB is an advance from a low point A to a high point B, this is recognized as a section upward. If a downward correction begins from point B, it is primarily taking place as a reaction to the preceding move. Wherever the correction ends can be labeled point C. When the uptrend resumes, you will have a couple ways to project price action.

The first is to calculate the new strength only in relation to the initial first section up. To give you the correct visual, Figure 3.5 shows what the A-B-C move might look like, with eighths retracements overlaying it.

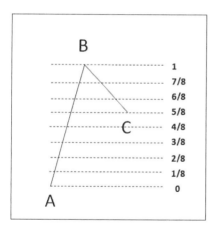

Figure 3.5 AB eighths retracements showing ABC

Figure 3.6 projects the entire set of eighths retracements from point B.

If you apply this method of projections to any of your charts, you will start to uncover which primary sections are capturing the rhythm of that particular market, and you will come to see that the projected resistances are useful in uncovering price targets.

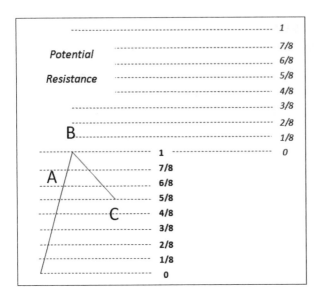

Figure 3.6 AB retracements projected from B

Figure 3.7 illustrates this method of retracement projection using a chart of Intel. The initial set of retracements was drawn from $17.60 (August 31, 2010), low point A, up to $22.21 (February 18, 2011), high point B. After retracing to $19.36 (April 4, 2011 low), just over 19.33, the 62.5% retracement, the stock resumed its uptrend and broke higher. The projection of the initial set of retracements was added to the chart. As you can clearly see, the projected retracements provided several useful points of resistance over the next eight months. The high at $23.96 (May 18, 2011) tested the projected 37.5% retracement at 23.94. The lower high at $23.39 (July 7, 2011) tested the projected 25% retracement at 23.36. The $22.98 pivot high (September 27, 2011) pierced the projected 12.5% retracement at 22.79. Continuing higher, the $24.50 pivot high (October 19, 2011) approached the projected 50% retracement at 24.52. The $25.20 high (October 27, 2011) tested the projected 62.5% retracement at 25.09. Lastly, of the projected retracement levels shown, the $25.78 high (December 7, 2011) was posted after a test of the projected 75% retracement at 25.67.

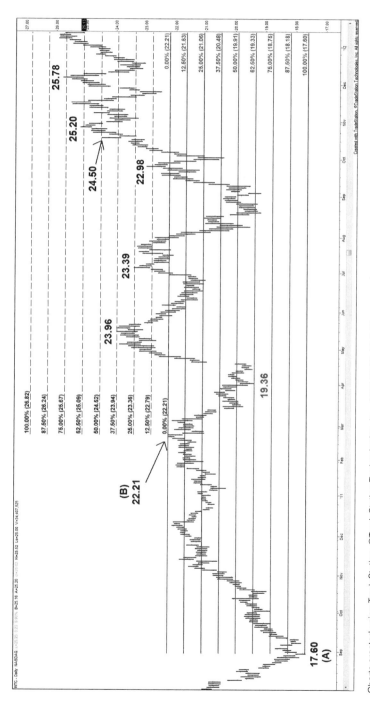

Charts created using TradeStation. ©TradeStation Technologies, Inc. 2001-2012. All rights reserved.

Figure 3.7 INTC, daily, as of January 24, 2012

The second method to project future price action from the A-B-C pattern is to calculate new strength in relation to the initial first section up *from* the correction itself. Here you would project the entire set of eighths retracements from point C, as shown in Figure 3.8.

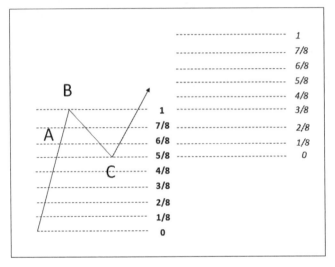

Figure 3.8 AB retracements projected from C

Figure 3.9 of AUDUSD (Australian dollar/U.S. dollar) illustrates this second method of retracement projection. The initial set of retracements was drawn from $0.6008 (October 27, 2010), low point A, up to $0.9405 (November 16, 2009), high point B. The market corrected to $0.8067 (May 25, 2010 low), probing the 37.5% retracement at 0.8131. The market then proceeded higher, and a set of retracements was projected from the $0.8067 pivot low. When the market broke out above the $0.9405 swing high, you can again clearly see how the projected retracements provided resistance, showing that the rhythm of the A-B-C move remained in play. $1.0182 (November 5, 2010 high) approached the projected 62.5% retracement at 1.0189. $1.0256 (December 31, 2010 high) then pierced the 1.0189 projected retracement level. $1.1011 (May 2, 2011 high) approached the projected 87.5% retracement at 1.1038. And $1.1080 (July 27, 2011 high) probed above the 1.1038 projected retracement level.

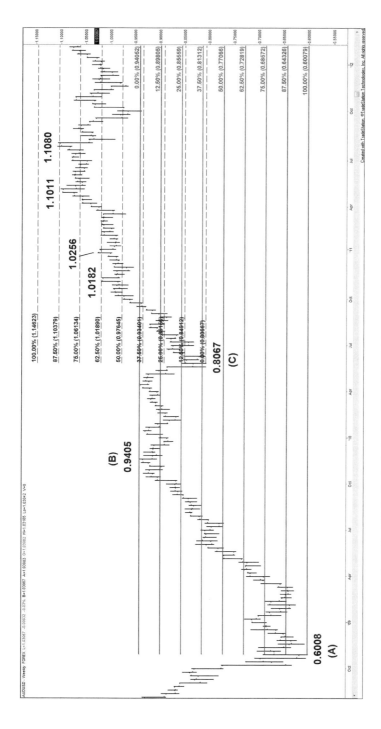

Charts created using TradeStation. ©TradeStation Technologies, Inc. 2001-2012. All rights reserved.

Figure 3.9 AUDUSD, weekly, as of January 20, 2012

Either of these methods of projecting retracement levels can also project support. However, prices generally have a floor at zero points, or zero dollars, and so forth. Therefore, the usefulness of projected retracement support relates directly to how high the level is from which prices are being projected.

You now have an understanding of the most basic ways Gann discovered support and resistance in his markets. As you practice measuring retracements as well as projecting retracements, you will get a feel for how to apply these tools most effectively.

4

Trading the Market

As I've observed market movement and made trades over the years, I have come to discover that every trade breaks down into eight distinct phases:

1. Trend assessment
2. Signal observation
3. Risk assessment
4. Order placement
5. Trade initiation
6. Trade management
7. Trade exit
8. Review

This chapter explores the phases of trend assessment and signal observation.

Trend assessment is the process of determining whether buyers or sellers are in command of the market. The illustrations of bull and bear market sections in Chapter 2 present a rough idea of how these trends develop. A bull campaign, as Gann would say, is more commonly known as an advance or uptrend. Similarly, a bear campaign is known as a decline or downtrend. An uptrend is most simply defined as a situation in which the market is making higher highs and higher lows. A downtrend is in place when the market is making lower highs and lower lows.

As trends unfold and change, a trader can profit consistently by recognizing buying and selling opportunities. However, not all signals to buy or sell are equal. Gann makes it very clear in his works that certain buy signals or sell signals, or "buying points" and "selling points," as he sometimes wrote, are more important than others.

Therefore, I introduce you to several of Gann's explicit buying and selling points, relative to their order of importance, which I've come to ascertain through repeated study.

Years ago, when I first read Gann's books and was trying to make his methodologies my own, I realized that I had a very graphic brain and would best embrace the points presented if I could translate them into illustrations. So I read and studied the rules, drew the figures, and collected examples of how the signals worked in real time, on my securities and time frames. In this chapter, I revisit my exercise in illustrating some of Gann's buying and selling points, but I use more up-to-date market examples.

The exact buying and selling points that I quote come from pages 39–41 of Gann's book *How to Make Profits Trading in Commodities.* They are also listed in Appendix C, "Gann's Buying and Selling Points." The examples used are marked with text directly relating to Gann's signal descriptions.

Several affirmative Gann rules can help you keep your focus on the right path as you explore the signals and examples:

Gann Rule (Affirmative) #7: Trade only in active markets.

By this, I believe that Gann was advising to trade in markets that have active participation. When you put on a trade, you want to be sure that your order can be easily filled based on the market's volume (or open interest).

Gann Rule (Affirmative) #5: Trade with the trend. Buy or sell only if you are sure of the trend, according to your chart and rules.

Gann Rule (Affirmative) #12: Trade the swings in accordance with the existing trend. This is where you can make the most profit for the fewest trades.

Gann Rule (Affirmative) #17: Trade only when you have definite signals.

Gann Rule (Affirmative) #18: Be just as willing to sell short as you are to buy. Let your object be to keep with the trend and make money.

Gann Rule (Affirmative) #19: Buy only when you have definite indication of a rising market. Sell only when you have definite indication of a falling market.

These five rules are all about tuning in to what the market is telling you. Know the trend (market direction). Know the signals for buying and selling. When they fall into place and you have a definite indication, *that* is the time to trade.

The buying and selling points are presented in several categories. Again, I share these in what I believe to be the order of descending importance.

Exceeding Moves in Time

Gann Buying Point #4: BUY when the first rally from the extreme bottom exceeds in time the greatest rally in the preceding Bear Campaign.

In Figure 4.1, T (stands for time) represents the duration of the greatest rally in the bear campaign shown. < T shows that the other rallies in the decline did not last as long as rally T. The signal to look for is when the rally off the low (after a three- or four-section bear campaign) takes more time to develop than T, hence the annotation >T.

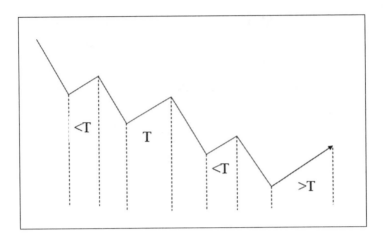

Figure 4.1 Gann Buying Point #4

Figure 4.2 shows Pitney Bowes on a weekly time frame. The decline from $73.31 (April 27, 1999 high) to $24.00 (December 16, 1999 low) consists of many rallies, large and small. Looking at the size of each rally in terms of time, the greatest rally occurred when the market rose from $40.88 (December 16, 1999 low) to $54.13 (March 2, 2000 high), spanning 12 weeks. The first rally from $24.00 reached $38.40 (February 15, 2001 high) before any substantial pullback took hold. The duration of this first rally, at 20 weeks, clearly exceeded the greatest rally in the preceding bear campaign.

> **Gann Selling Point #4**: SELL after the first decline exceeds the greatest reaction in the preceding Bull Campaign or the last reaction before final top.

To keep this selling point in line with the similar buying point, I focus on the *greatest* reaction (instead of the last reaction). In Figure 4.3, T represents the duration of the greatest correction lower within the bull campaign shown. < T shows that the other corrections in the advance did not last as long as correction T. The signal to look for is when the decline from the high (after a three- or four-section bull campaign) takes more time to develop than T, hence the annotation >T.

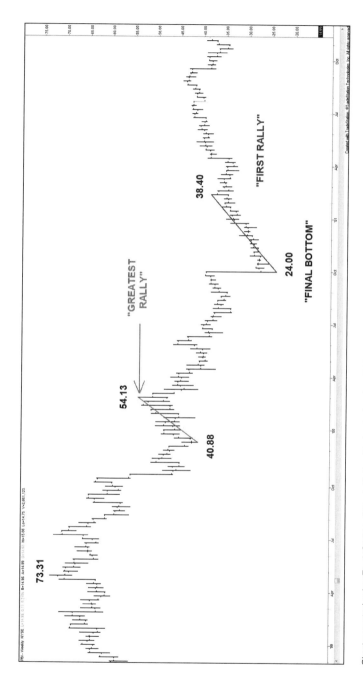

Charts created using TradeStation. ©TradeStation Technologies, Inc. 2001-2012. All rights reserved.

Figure 4.2 PBI, weekly, as of November 9, 2001

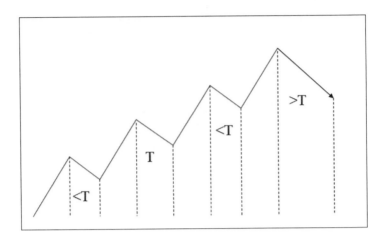

Figure 4.3 Gann Selling Point #4

Figure 4.4 revisits the Google chart that Chapter 2, "Elements of the Market," explored. The rally from $247.30 (November 21, 2008 low) to $629.51 (January 4, 2010 high) consists of many corrections, small and large. Looking at the size of each correction in terms of time, the greatest reaction occurred when the market fell from $447.34 (June 5, 2009 high) to $395.98 (July 7, 2009 low), spanning 32 days. The first decline from $629.51 reached $520.00 (February 25, 2010) before any substantial correction took hold. The duration of this first decline, at 52 days, clearly exceeded the greatest reaction in the preceding bull campaign.

The next pair of Buying and Selling Points focuses on the final rally/reaction in the preceding trend move.

> **Gann Buying Point #5**: BUY when the period of time exceeds the last rally before extreme lows were reached. If the last rally was 3 or 4 weeks, when the advance from the bottom is more than 3 or 4 weeks, consider the trend has turned up and commodities are a safer buy on a secondary reaction.

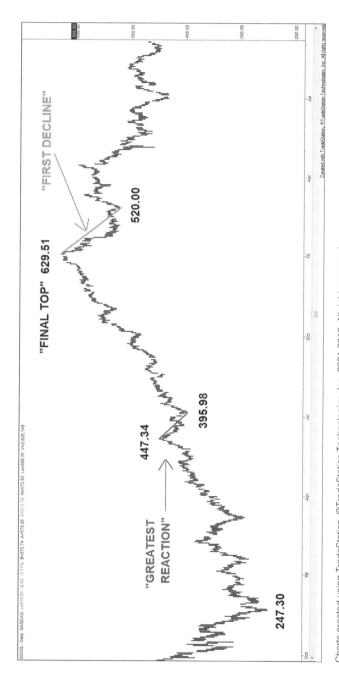

Charts created using TradeStation. ©TradeStation Technologies, Inc. 2001-2012. All rights reserved.

Figure 4.4 GOOG, daily, as of September 3, 2010

In Figure 4.5, T represents the duration of the final rally in the bear campaign shown. The signal to look for is when the rally off the low (after a three- or four-section bear campaign) takes more time to develop than the latest rally, hence the annotation >T.

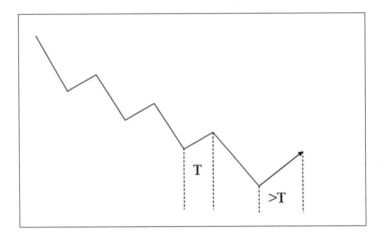

Figure 4.5 Gann Buying Point #5

Figure 4.6 displays the S&P 500 Cash Index. The market declined from 1219.80 (April 26, 2010 high) to 1010.91 (July 1, 2010 low). The first leg of the rally from the 1010.91 low lasted 13 days (calendar), akin to the previous rally from 1042.17 (June 8, 2010 low) to 1131.23 (June 21, 2010 high), which lasted 14 days. However, the market continued rising off 1010.91 for a total of 41 calendar days, posting a high at 1129.24 (August 9, 2010 high). The 41-day period exceeded the last rally from 1042.17 to 1131.23 (14 days). A reversal from 1129.24 was seen to the downside, and a secondary reaction came in at 1039.70 (August 27, 2010 low), testing 1040.49, the 75% retracement of the 1010.91/1129.24 move up.

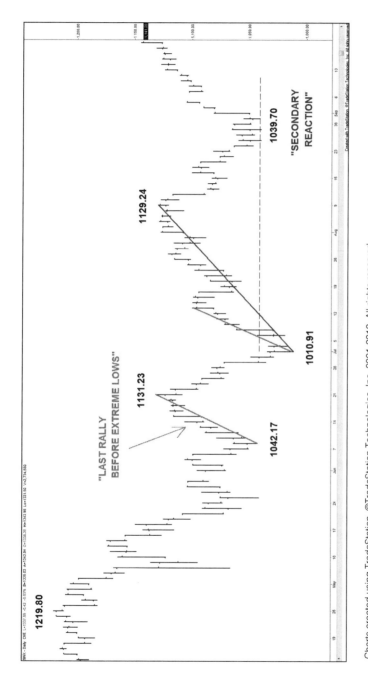

Charts created using TradeStation. ©TradeStation Technologies, Inc. 2001-2012. All rights reserved.

Figure 4.6 $INX, daily, as of September 20, 2010

Gann Selling Point #6: Sell when the period of time of the first decline exceeds the last reaction before final top of the Bull Campaign. Example: If wheat or any commodity has advanced for several months or for one year or more, and the greatest reaction has been 4 weeks, which is an average reaction in a Bull Market, then after top is reached and the first decline runs more than 4 weeks, it is an indication of a change in the minor trend or the main trend. The commodity will be a safer short sale on any rally because you will be trading with the trend after it has been definitely defined.

In Figure 4.7, T represents the duration of the final correction lower within the bull campaign shown. The signal to look for is when the move lower from the high (after a three- or four-section bull campaign) takes more time to develop than the final correction T, hence the annotation >T.

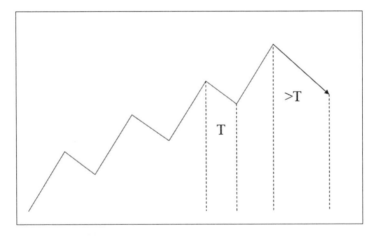

Figure 4.7 Gann Selling Point #6

Figure 4.8 shows a weekly chart of Cisco Systems. The market rallied from $13.61 (March 9, 2009 low) to $27.74 (April 30, 2010 high). At first, the decline from the $27.74 high lasted 4 weeks, akin to the previous reaction from $25.10 (January 15, 2010 high) to $22.35 (January 28, 2010 low), which lasted 3 weeks. However, the market continued lower from $27.74 for a total of 10 weeks, posting a low at $20.93 (July 1, 2010). The period of time (10 weeks) had exceeded the "last reaction" before extreme highs were reached (3 weeks). A reversal from $27.74 was seen to the upside, and a secondary rally came in at $24.87 (August 9, 2010 high).

Triple Bottoms/Tops

> **Gann Rule (Affirmative) #25:** Let the market prove it is making a top. Let the market prove it is making a bottom. By following definite rules, you can do this.

Although triple bottoms and tops (and double bottoms and tops, to be explored) are known and studied within the realm of technical analysis in general, they are formations that were very important to Gann and deserve exploration from what I perceived to be his point of view through my repeated study.

> **Gann Buying Point #8:** BUY against double or **triple bottoms**, or buy on first, second, or third higher bottom and buy a second lot after wheat, soybeans, or cotton makes second or third higher bottom, then crosses previous top.

This particular Buying Point has several elements to it. I focus on the triple bottom.

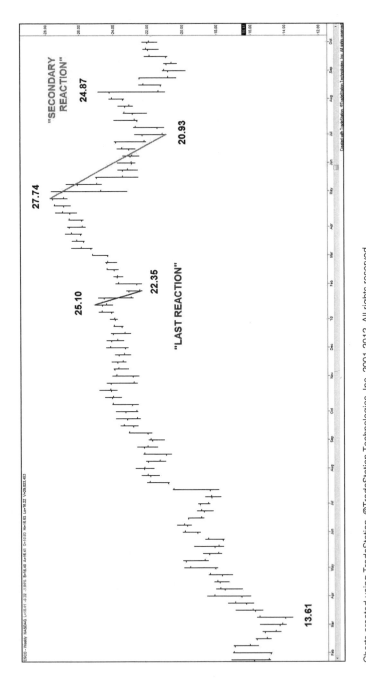

Figure 4.8 CSCO, weekly, as of September 24, 2010

Figure 4.9 illustrates a triple bottom. The greater the amount of time between the lows of the triple bottom, the more significant the following move.

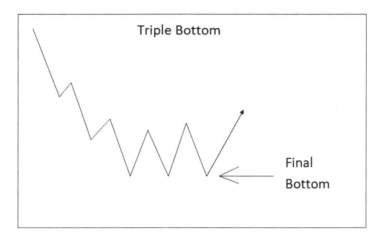

Figure 4.9 Triple bottom

Figure 4.10 explores a weekly chart of Transocean, Ltd. The market made a low at $18.10 (October 10, 2002). The market then approached the same low, reaching $18.40 on May 1, 2003. Attempts were seen on that area of support a few months later, and the final low was posted at $18.49 (November 4, 2003) before the market broke out above the formation. This example of a triple bottom is valuable because it shows a textbook version of the formation, in which the peaks in between the lows are also near each other. This is not crucial to trading the pattern, but it does define a clearer boundary for a breakout.

Another significance of this triple bottom is its duration. The first low to the third low was about 13 months. Remember, the longer the duration of the topping or bottoming formation, the more significant the subsequent price action. In this case (not shown on chart), the subsequent advance lasted 30 months, topping at $90.16 (May 11, 2006 high).

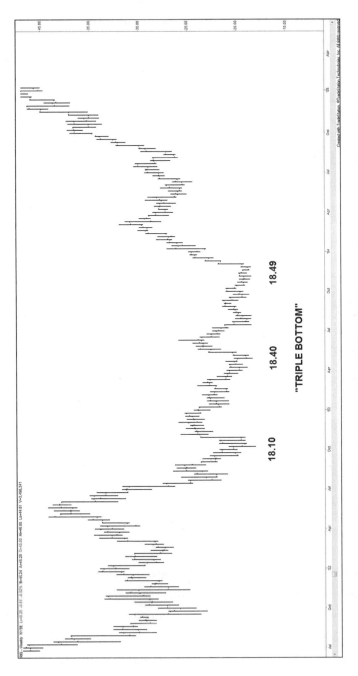

Charts created using TradeStation. ©TradeStation Technologies, Inc. 2001-2012. All rights reserved.

Figure 4.10 RIG, weekly, as of December 3, 2004

Gann Selling Point #8: SELL against double tops or **triple tops**, or SELL when the market makes lower tops or lower bottoms. It is safe to sell when wheat, soybeans, or cotton makes a second, third, or fourth lower top, also safe to sell after *double* and *triple bottoms* are broken.

Figure 4.11 illustrates a triple top. Triple tops tend to be shorter in duration than triple bottoms. Why? Well, for starters, a triple bottom is a variation of a phase of accumulation. Greed fuels accumulation. A triple top is a variation of a phase of distribution. Fear is the driving force behind distribution. Man's fear is stronger than man's greed. Fear builds more quickly than greed. Therefore, the lower boundary of a topping pattern such as the triple top is likely to be traded through more quickly than the upper boundary of a triple bottom.

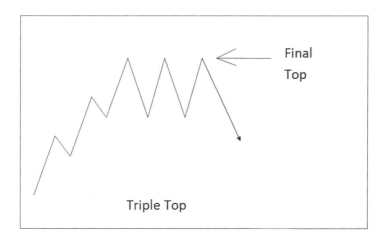

Figure 4.11 Triple Top

Now, despite the fact that triple tops tend to span less time than triple bottoms, time plays an important role in their analysis. As with triple bottoms, the greater the amount of time between the highs of a triple top, the more significant the following move.

Figure 4.12 revisits the Micron Technology chart that Chapter 2 explored. The market made a high at $11.95 (February 14, 2011) and then approached the same high 6 weeks later, reaching $11.89 on March 30, 2011. The last attempt at that area was seen a month after that, on April 27, 2011, with the high posting at $11.83 before the market tumbled. This particular example of a triple top is valuable because it shows the variations that can occur within the formation but that indicate the same bearish sentiment. According to my illustration for a triple top, one might expect that all the highs must "match" for the pattern to be valid. However, what's more important is to look at the overall picture of the trend that the pattern is painting.

You might be wondering how to trade this formation. Take a look at Figure 4.13, which zooms in on the price action of the triple top area.

The first indication that the final top within a triple top might be forming came on April 29, 2011, when the market broke below higher bar lows at $11.24 (April 21, 2011) and $11.25 (April 25, 2011). The market then moved lower before a small rebound came in, which was capped at $11.13 (May 6, 2011). This would have been an area for an aggressive sell entry.

The market then continued lower toward the $10.26 pivot low (April 18, 2011). Since this was one of the troughs within the pattern of the triple top, waiting for the break of this low before selling would have been safer than selling based on the earlier break of the $11.24/$11.25 bar lows. The market made its first substantial (closing basis) break below $10.26 on May 17, 2011, and a small rebound to $10.21 appeared. This would have been an area for a safer sell entry.

Finally, the last level to watch to confirm the triple top was the trough at $9.65 (March 10, 2011). The market broke below this level on May 23, 2011, and continued lower for a couple days before a rebound took place. The rebound capped at $10.23 (May 31, 2011). This would have been the area for the safest sell entry following the triple top formation.

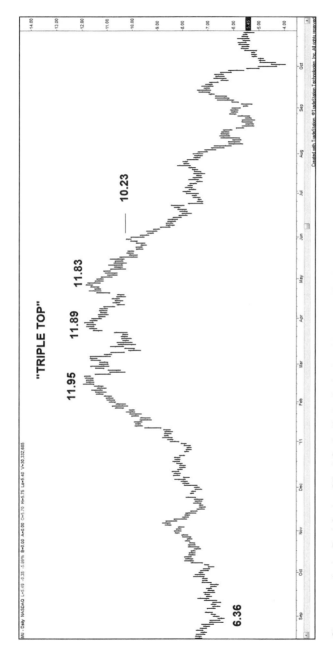

Charts created using TradeStation. ©TradeStation Technologies, Inc. 2001-2012. All rights reserved.

Figure 4.12 MU, daily, as of October 25, 2011

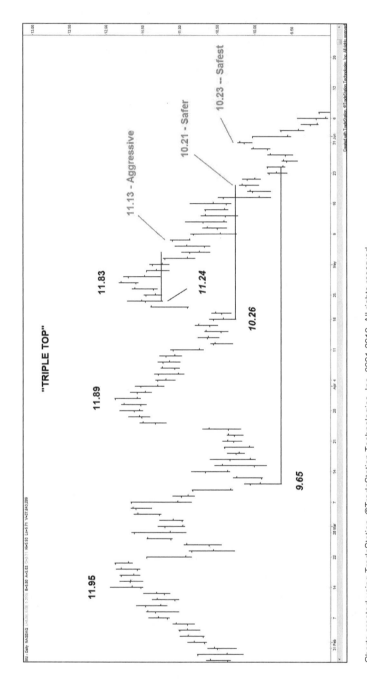

Figure 4.13 MU, daily, as of June 7, 2011

Double Bottoms/Tops

Gann Buying Point #8: BUY against **double** or triple **bottoms** ....

Once again, this particular buying point has several elements to it. I now focus on double bottoms, as illustrated in Figure 4.14.

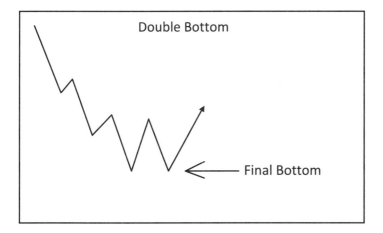

Figure 4.14 Double bottom

Figure 4.15 shows America Movil stock on a weekly time frame. The decline from $34.58 (October 18, 2007 high) lasted one year, reaching a low of $11.59 (October 24, 2008). The market subsequently rebounded to $17.48 (January 6, 2009 high). The return move lower reached $11.68 (March 2, 2009 low), forming a pivot that was the first indication of a double bottom. The stock then rallied back through the $17.48 swing high, confirming the double bottom pattern. Note that it took 20 weeks for the double bottom to form. The greater the time between the lows, the more significant the low is; this became apparent as the advance from the double bottom lows extended to last about 2 years.

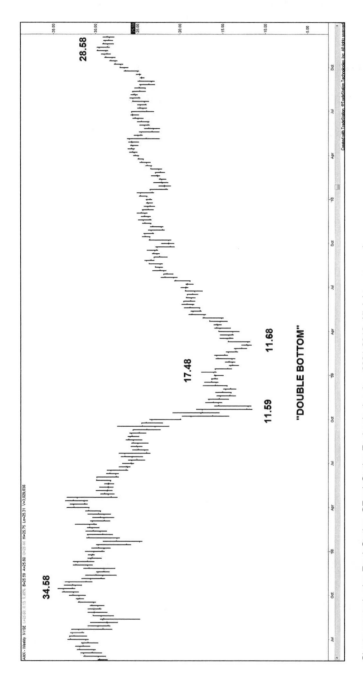

Charts created using TradeStation. ©TradeStation Technologies, Inc. 2001-2012. All rights reserved.

Figure 4.15 AMX, weekly, as of December 10, 2010

Similar to how I explained the possible entries on a triple top, I highlight the possible entry points on this double bottom. Take a look at Figure 4.16, which moves to a daily chart to zoom in on the price action of the double bottom area.

The first indication that the final bottom within a double bottom might be forming came on March 12, 2009, when the market broke above the lower bar high at $13.03 (February 26, 2009). The market then moved higher before a correction came in, which held at $13.13 (March 30, 2009 low). This would have been an area for an aggressive buy entry.

The market then continued higher toward the $15.96 pivot high (February 10, 2009). Because this was a swing high within the context of the pattern of the double bottom, waiting for the break of this high before buying would have been safer than buying based on the earlier break of the $13.03 bar high. The market made its first substantial break (closing basis) above $15.96 on April 24, 2009, and then a small correction to $14.94 (April 27, 2009) appeared. This would have been an area for a safer buy entry.

Finally, the last level to watch to confirm the double bottom was the peak at $17.48. The market broke above this level on May 4, 2009, and continued higher for a few days before a correction took hold. The correction based at $17.52 (May 15, 2009). This would have been the area for the safest buy entry following the double bottom formation.

Note that the market ended up breaking below the $17.52 pivot low to reach $17.39 (June 23, 2009 low) before resuming higher. If you had been long from either one of the $13.13 or $14.94 areas, you probably would have collected your profit and been positioned to re-enter the market long. If you had gotten long around $17.52, you would have probably taken a small loss and been out from the position. However, the market always makes it clear when it is giving you a second chance to get in on the trend. Keep an eye out for this as you apply any of these buying and selling points in real time.

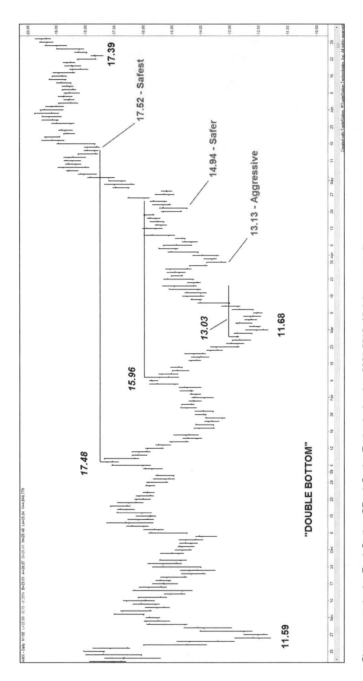

Figure 4.16 AMX, daily, as of June 30, 2009

Gann Selling Point #8: SELL against **Double Tops** or Triple Tops....

Figure 4.17 illustrates a double top.

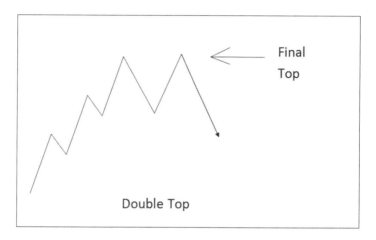

Figure 4.17 Double top

Figure 4.18 looks at the advance in Micron Technology from late 2008 to early 2010. The advance from the $1.59 low (November 20, 2008) put in a high at $11.34 (January 6, 2010). A correction forming a swing low appeared, but the subsequent rally reached only $11.40 (April 4, 2010 high). This was the first indication that a double top might be forming. The break lower to $7.32 (May 6, 2010) confirmed the formation. As with the triple top formation example, there would have been multiple points of entry. Also to note here that it took three months to form this double top, adding to the significance of it in terms of the subsequent downward move.

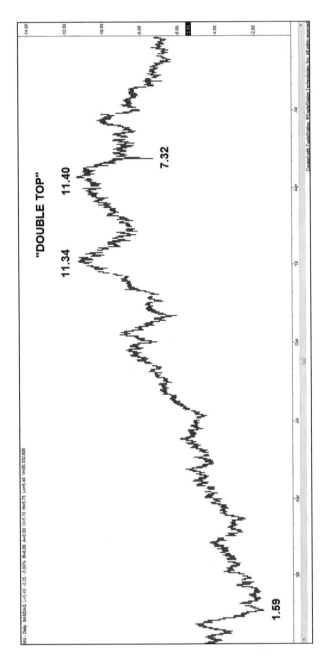

Figure 4.18 MU, daily, as of September 22, 2010

Exceeding Moves in Price

Gann Buying Point #3: SAFEST BUYING POINT. Buy on a secondary reaction after wheat, cotton, or any commodity has crossed previous weekly tops and the advance exceeds the greatest rally on the way down from the top.

In Figure 4.19, P represents the price range in points/cents of the greatest rally in the bear campaign shown. < P shows that the other rallies in the decline were not as large as rally P. The signal to look for is when the rally off the low (after a three- or four-section bear campaign) exceeds in size the greatest rally P. The safest time to enter long is when the market has pulled back afterward, creating a higher low (secondary reaction).

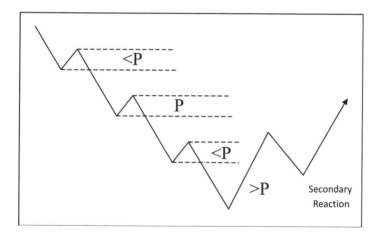

Figure 4.19 Gann Buying Point #3

Although Gann talks about "weekly" price action, I have come to see how his buying and selling points span all time frames. Figure 4.20 display a daily chart of the stock Honeywell International.

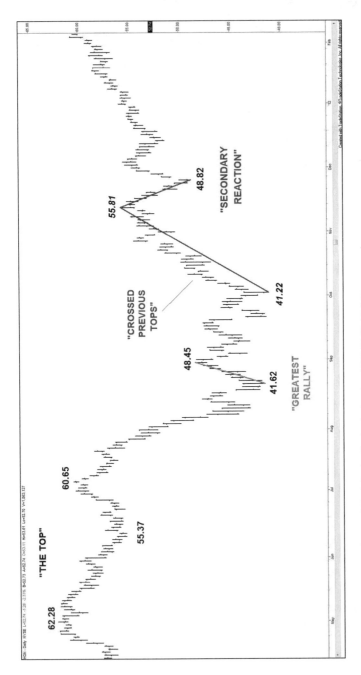

Figure 4.20 HON, daily, as of February 7, 2012

Here you can see that Honeywell declined from the top at $62.28 (May 2, 2011) to the low at $41.22 (October 4, 2011). Along the way, the greatest rally took place near the low, from $41.62 (August 22, 2011) to $48.45 (August 31, 2011). The market crossed the previous top at $48.45 on October 12, 2011. The breakout reached a high of $55.81 (November 11, 2011) before any major reaction was seen. The safest buying point, the secondary reaction, then came in and found support at $48.82 (November 25, 2011), very close to $48.52, the 50% retracement of the $41.22/$55.81 section up.

> **Gann Selling Point #3**: SAFEST SELLING POINT. Sell on a *secondary rally* after wheat, soybeans, cotton, or any commodity has broken the previous bottoms of several weeks or has broken the bottom of the last reaction, turning trend down. This *secondary rally* nearly always comes after the first sharp decline in the first section of the Bear Campaign.

In Figure 4.21, P represents the price range in points/cents of the greatest correction in the bull campaign shown. < P shows that the other corrections during the advance were not as large as correction P. The signal to look for is when the pullback from the high (after a three- or four-section bull campaign) exceeds in size the greatest correction P. The safest time to enter short is when the market has started to recover, creating a higher low (secondary reaction).

Figure 4.22 displays a daily chart of Juniper Networks. You can see that the stock rallied from the bottom at $12.09 (August 11, 2006) to the high at $37.95 (October 9, 2007).

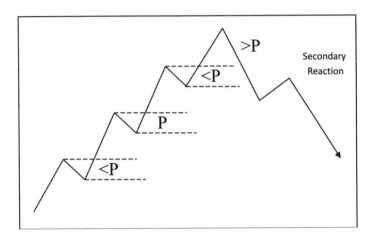

Figure 4.21 Gann Selling Point #3

Moving to Figure 4.23, which zooms in on the end phase of that advance, you can see that the last move higher rose from $28.61 (August 16, 2007 low), making it the bottom of the last reaction. This level was pierced with the fall to $28.01 on November 21, 2007, indicating that bulls were no longer in complete control. The safest selling point, the secondary reaction, came in at $34.95 (December 24, 2007 high).

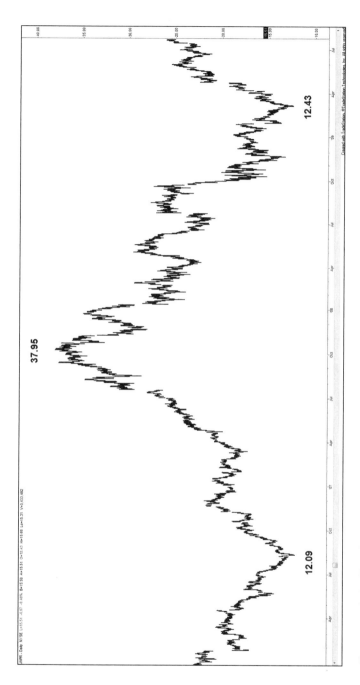

Charts created using TradeStation. ©TradeStation Technologies, Inc. 2001-2012. All rights reserved.

Figure 4.22 JNPR, daily, as of July 23, 2009

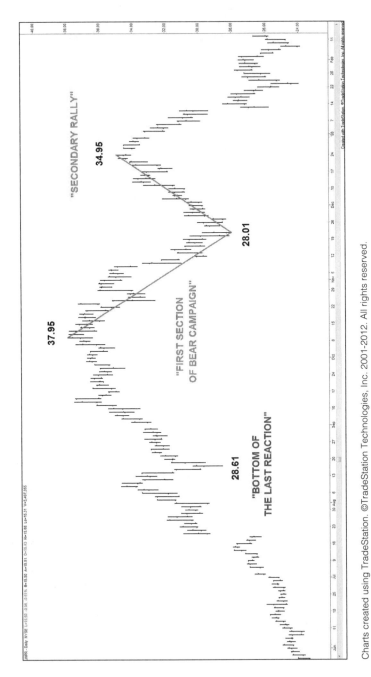

Charts created using TradeStation. ©TradeStation Technologies, Inc. 2001-2012. All rights reserved.

Figure 4.23 JNPR, daily, as of February 11, 2008

Buy Old Tops/Sell Old Bottoms

> **Gann Buying Point #1**: BUY at OLD BOTTOMS or **OLD TOP** .... Buy when ... any commodity ... declines 1 cent to 3 cents under old tops or bottoms.

I have truncated this buying point to get to the core of it, and I do so with the relative selling point. Appendix C presents more text.

Although Figure 4.24 is a rough sketch and is not drawn to scale, I intentionally drew three different versions of buying at old tops, derived from Gann's descriptions:

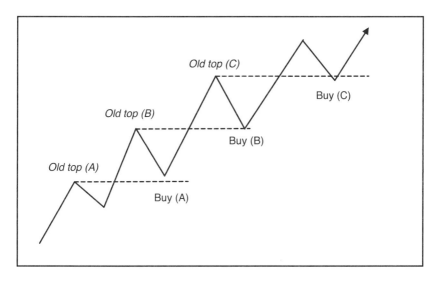

Figure 4.24 Gann Buying Point #1

Old top (A)/Buy (A) illustrates how holding slightly higher than these old levels is the strongest indication to the upside.

Old top (B)/Buy (B) illustrates how holding at these levels and not breaking under is also a strong indication.

Finally, Old top (C)/Buy (C) illustrates when the market dips just below the previous tops. This is the weakest of the three variations of buying at old tops, but it can still provide easy-to-find, low-risk opportunities to enter long in an uptrend.

Figure 4.25 shows a weekly chart of Gap, Inc., advancing from a double bottom at $9.41 (November 20, 2008 low)/$9.56 (March 6, 2009 low). The market rose to $18.76 (June 1, 2009) before correcting back toward the old top at $14.57 (December 8, 2009). The market failed to reach the old top, akin to the Old top (A)/Buy (A) example in Figure 2.4. This reinforced the strength of the new uptrend, and a pivot low formed at $14.65 (July 9, 2009 low). From there, the market broke higher to reach $23.36 (October 19, 2009 high). The correction off that high retested the old top at $18.76, pushing slightly below that level, akin to the Old top (C)/Buy (C) example in Figure 2.4. The market then formed a higher pivot low at $18.64 (January 25, 2010 low).

Gann Selling Point #1: SELL at OLD TOPS or OLD BOTTOMS ....

Figure 4.26 shows three different versions of selling at old bottoms, derived from Gann's descriptions:

Old bottom (A)/Sell (A) shows how, when the market is very weak, rallies stop right under the old bottoms before the downtrend resumes.

Old bottom (B)/Sell (B) illustrates how holding at the old bottom level is also a good indication of the weakness of the market.

Finally, Old bottom (C)/Sell (C) illustrates when the market rallies just above the old bottoms. Depending on how far up the market goes and where it trades from there, this might indicate strength. However, if the market turns back below the old bottom soon after probing above it, this can provide easy-to-find, low-risk opportunities to enter short in a downtrend.

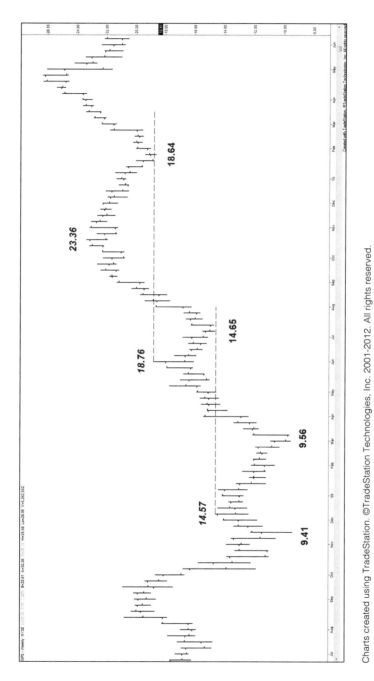

Charts created using TradeStation. ©TradeStation Technologies, Inc. 2001-2012. All rights reserved.

Figure 4.25 GPS, weekly, as of June 11, 2010

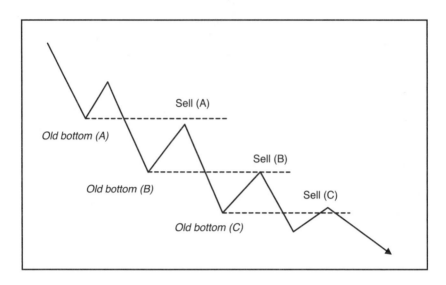

Figure 4.26 Gann Selling Point #1

The following market example illustrates a couple of these types of rallies to old bottoms.

Figure 4.27 shows a daily chart of Clearwire Corporation. The stock initiated a downtrend off the $8.82 high (September 30, 2010) with the break below $5.99 (July 20, 2010 low). The market fell to $4.63 (December 21, 2010 low) before rallying back toward the old bottom at $5.99. The first test of the old bottom was on January 6, 2011, posting a high at $6.00 (shown on chart). This is akin to Old bottom (B)/Sell (B) as illustrated in Figure 4.26. The market then consolidated for a few months, but the entire range was capped by tests of the $5.99 old bottom, which provided several short opportunities: $6.00 again (February 4), $5.98 (February 14), $5.95 (March 11), and finally $6.11 on April 7, 2011 (shown on chart).

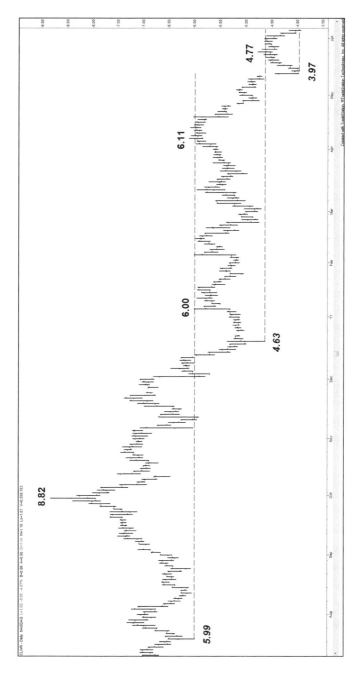

Charts created using TradeStation. ©TradeStation Technologies, Inc. 2001-2012. All rights reserved.

Figure 4.27 CLWR, daily, as of June 3, 2011

Figure 4.28 focuses on the price action following the $6.11 high. As you can see, selling old bottoms is effective on the day-to-day swings within the greater daily chart swings. The first instance is the formation of the $5.19 high (May 4, 2011), which tested the $5.27 old bottom (April 20, 2011), akin to the Old bottom (A)/Sell (A) illustration in Figure 4.26 The market then declined to $3.97 (May 13, 2011 low). The subsequent rally marked a high at $4.77 (May 24, 2011). This tested the most recent old bottom at $4.75 (April 28, 2011), as well as the previously mentioned $4.63 swing low (represented by the dashed line).

The downtrend continued from $4.77, and this chart illustrates two more instances of selling at old bottoms. The first is the $4.35 lower high (June 8, 2011 high), which respected the $4.37 old bottom (May 26, 2011). Then the market formed a lower high at $3.90 (June 16, 2011), which respected the $3.94 old bottom (June 6, 2011).

Rapid Moves

Gann Buying Point #9: BUYING RULES FOR RAPID ADVANCES AT HIGH LEVELS. In the last stages of a Bull Market in a commodity, reactions are small. Buy on 2-day reactions and follow up with STOP LOSS ORDER 1 cent to 2 cents under each day's low level. Then when the low of a previous day is broken, you will be out. Markets sometimes run 10 to 30 days without breaking low of previous day.

Figure 4.29 illustrates the 2-day reaction. The trade action indicated by the circle illustrates the market correcting lower for two days before resuming higher to form a pivot low. This shows what a buy opportunity would resemble according to Buying Point #9.

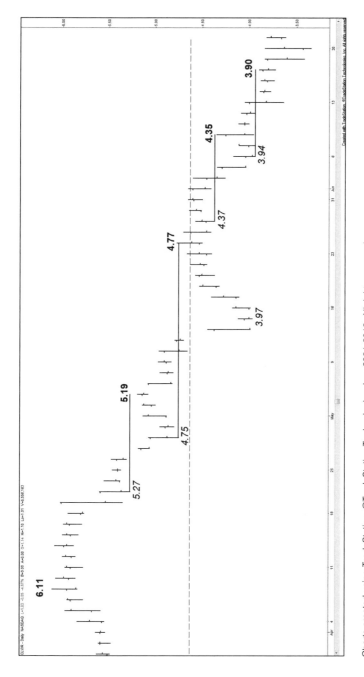

Charts created using TradeStation. ©TradeStation Technologies, Inc. 2001-2012. All rights reserved.

Figure 4.28 CLWR, daily, as of June 21, 2011

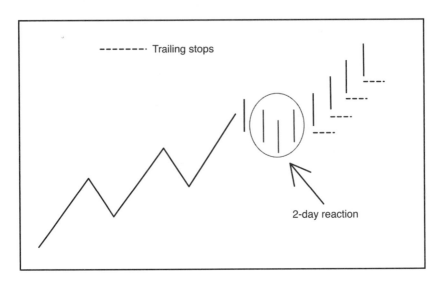

Figure 4.29 Gann Buying Point #9

The focus of the example in Figure 4.30 is on the last sentence from the buying point: "Markets sometimes run 10 to 30 days without breaking low of previous day." The daily chart of soybean futures (July 2012 contract) shows that the market broke higher from consolidation on February 13, 2012. A higher low formed at $12.63 (February 16) before the market ran up to $13.31 3/4 (February 29). This was a run of 9 trading days during which each day's higher low level remained intact.

> **Gann Selling Point #9**: SELL in the last stages of Bear Market or when there is rapid decline and only 2 days' rallies, and follow down with stop loss order 1 cent above the high of the previous day. When wheat or any commodity rallies 1 cent or more above the high of the previous day, you will be out on *stop*. Fast-declining markets will often run 10 to 30 days without crossing the high of the previous day.

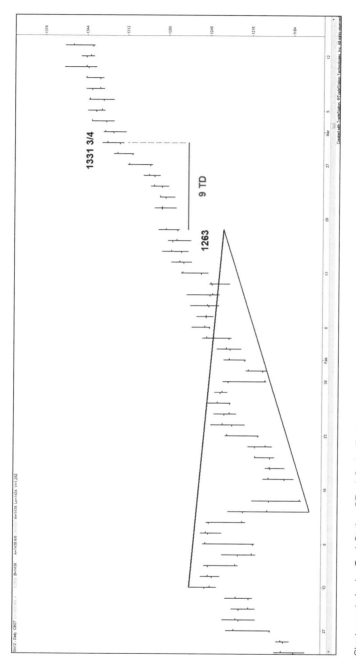

Charts created using TradeStation. ©TradeStation Technologies, Inc. 2001–2012. All rights reserved.

Figure 4.30 SN12, daily, as of March 3, 2012

Figure 4.31 illustrates the 2-day rally. The trade action indicated by the circle illustrates the market correcting higher for two days before resuming lower to form a pivot high. This shows what a sell opportunity would resemble according to Selling Point #9.

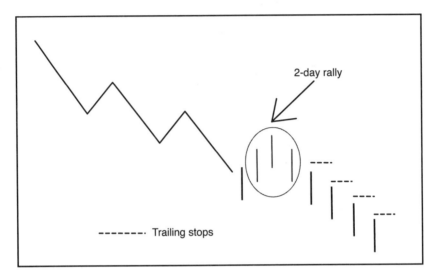

Figure 4.31 Gann Selling Point #9

As with the corresponding buying point, this example focuses on the last sentence of the selling point: "Fast-declining markets will often run 10 to 30 days without crossing the high of the previous day."

Figure 4.32 again shows the July 2012 soybean futures chart. You can see that the market formed a lower high at $14.53 3/4 on September 12, 2011. The market plummeted lower to $12.59 1/4 (September 26, 2011 low). This was a run of 11 trading days during which each day's lower high level remained intact.

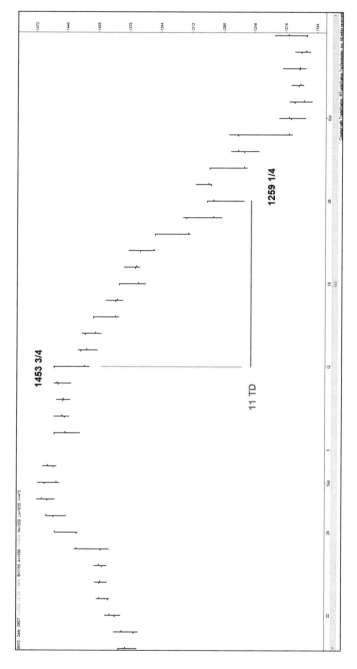

Charts created using TradeStation. ©TradeStation Technologies, Inc. 2001-2012. All rights reserved.

Figure 4.32 SN12, daily, as of October 10, 2011

Trading Ranges

The market is always trading in an uptrend, downtrend, or sideways. At first glance, it might seem that Gann's trading points are best applied only to clear uptrends and downtrends. After all, according to him, that's where the greatest profits lie. However, when the market is trading sideways, it doesn't mean that the market is not tradable. In fact, opportunities to follow Gann's basic buying and selling points still appear repeatedly, providing trade opportunities. What changes is the management of the trade and perhaps even the duration from entry to exit.

Three basic types of sideways price movement take place. The first occurs when range trading occurs at low levels in the market relative to the previous trend. In these situations, **accumulation** is taking place. Figure 4.33 illustrates what happens when large investors build up their long positions in a security before removing a ceiling so that prices can surge higher.

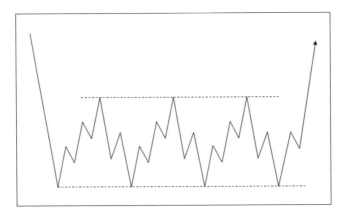

Figure 4.33 Accumulation

Figure 4.33 is an approximation of the types of price movements that occur within a base (range of accumulation). Generally, the upward price moves occur on greater volume (or open interest, for commodities) than the downward moves. The structures of the upward price moves might even resemble three or four sections up, and the downward moves might resemble corrections. Clear boundaries generally form on both sides of the range; they may be straight across, as in this figure, or they may slant toward each other (converging boundaries) or away from each other (diverging boundaries).

Another key point to note about accumulation is that the longer the duration of the accumulation phase, the more significant the subsequent breakout. Every subset of sections and corrections within an accumulation phase can be compared to the tightening of a metal spring coil. When a boundary is broken and the "tension" is released, the subsequent market action reflects all the pent-up trading energy that was part of the accumulation process.

The second type of sideways price movement is called **distribution.** In this situation, range trading occurs at high levels relative to the previous trend. Figure 4.34 illustrates large investors decreasing their positions in a security before removing a price floor so that the market can drop lower.

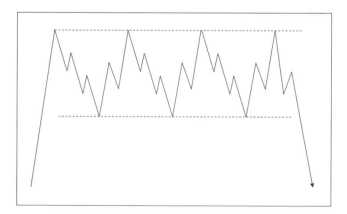

Figure 4.34 Distribution

Generally, completing a phase of distribution takes less time than completing a phase of accumulation. This is because the fear that is integral to distribution is stronger than the greed that fuels accumulation.

The third type of sideways price movement can occur during an uptrend or a downtrend. Many subsets of these types of sideways movements exist; they are generally continuation patterns (the prior trend eventually resumes). However, I want to examine at a seemingly random consolidation movement.

Figure 4.35 illustrates a general sideways series of price movements. However, looking closely at the delineated action, you can see that swing highs and swing lows are broken within the overall price action. One can apply the Gann buying and selling points when this scenario presents on live charts, making short-term trades and profiting off the sideways trend.

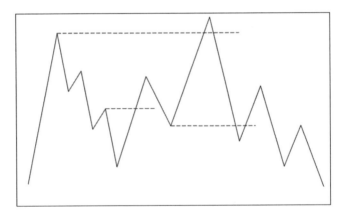

Figure 4.35 Random consolidation

Better yet is when the consolidation is not so seemingly random and actually has some clear boundaries to it. Figure 4.36 illustrates consolidation that creates definitive boundaries as it unfolds. The trend preceding the sideways action in this case is up. Therefore, the end of consolidation likely will result in the continuation of the uptrend, illustrated by the breakout at point A.

In an uptrend, consolidation patterns that imply continuation higher often have a downward slant. This makes sense because a consolidation pattern is really just a complex correction; therefore, it is likely to work against the prior trend. Similarly, in a downtrend, consolidation patterns that imply continuation lower often have an upward slant.

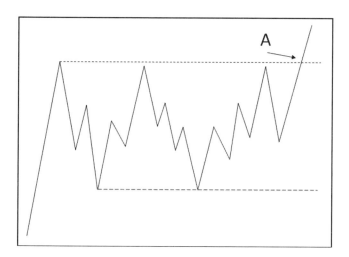

Figure 4.36 Consolidation with definitive boundaries

When attempting to participate in short-term trade opportunities *within* these boundaries, the best approach is to favor the "slant" of the consolidation, whatever direction that is. Most importantly, be aware of the direction of the preceding trend at all times so that you are better prepared for the eventual breakout.

By using Gann's principles to understand the inner workings of all these different episodes of sideways market action, you'll be able to capitalize on the short-term movements within these patterns and be ready for breakouts and subsequent trend moves.

5

Application of Gann's Principles

In this chapter, I present how I've made what Gann wrote my own. This practice is crucial to your continued study of Gann's works. You must be willing to mold and shape the principles Gann presents into different but related concepts. This is critical for two main reasons. First, Gann does not share his secrets easily, as you can see when reading his books. The second reason is that even though Gann wrote books and shared how he traded, we can never emulate exactly how he used the information he presented. We were not there to watch him move through his analysis routines, and we do not know how he ultimately made his trading decisions. Therefore, it is in our best interest to look at each tenet he shared from different angles.

Gann's Favorite Numbers

The earlier exploration of eighths retracements introduced the numbers and ratios that Gann found to be most significant in his study of the markets. Similar to how Gann prioritized buying and selling points, his writing made very clear what mathematical relationships in the market were more important than others. I explore some of these relationships, many which translate directly to types of support or resistance levels.

100% Retracement

The 100% retracement of the range from the extreme high to extreme low (or extreme low to extreme high) is a significant level because of human psychology. Many have debated whether the market has a memory and thus reacts to past high and low prices. But whether the market has a memory is not the issue. What's key is that the market is traded by human beings, and we definitely have memories. Whether we were actually trading as individuals when an extreme high or extreme low formed is inconsequential. Anyone trading a market can find a way to access the historical data and see the extreme high and low prices. Thus, our perception of "too high" and "too low" comes into play.

50% Retracement

The 50% concept is one we've already explored in this book. Gann presented the 50% retracement as important in several ways. In the first scenario, it was 50% of the range from the extreme high to the extreme low (main halfway point). The significance of this is direct enough. Another way Gann found 50% to be valuable was in a cluster of 50% retracements near the same level. He also found it of value when a 50% retracement was clustered with other retracements near the same level.

Taking this out a few steps, Gann emphasized the 50% level as the most important retracement within the eighths. We've seen retracements applied to swing highs and swing lows to find key supports and resistances, essentially measuring retracements within the element of price. Let's now look at the other elements present on a chart that can be measured by retracements: time, patterns, and reversal bars.

Figure 5.1 illustrates the concept of looking at 50% of time. The simplest approach is to look at the amount of time present within a move that can be analyzed for retracements. I've presented a low-to-high move with a duration of 10 days. Subsequent market action, while potentially showing significance at 50% of price, might also exhibit significant action at 50% of the time of the previous move. Fifty percent of 10 equals 5, so the 5-day retracement is projected forward to suggest significant price action at day 10, day 15, and so forth.

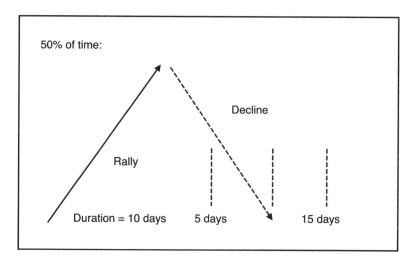

Figure 5.1 50% of time

This topic reminds me of the following question. Given that the market is not open every single day, and charts do not always account for weekends or holidays by keeping white space, should time calculations be measured according to calendar days or trading days? When I first pondered this issue, I realized that since this is an issue only on charts with a time frame of daily or intraday, perhaps it is best to start applying time analysis to charts with a time frame of weekly or greater. This would allow me to get a feel for market movement along the x-axis of time, which would be a new way of looking at things; as traders, we are generally more focused on the y-axis of price. If I then chose to return to charts with a time frame of daily or less for time analysis, I would be better able to compare the observations I made when measuring using calendar days versus trading days.

Figure 5.2 shows a weekly chart of Pfizer, Inc. The advance from $11.62 (March 2, 2009 low) to $20.36 (January 20, 2010 high) lasted 47 weeks. The market reversed lower off $20.36, and during the 24th week of the move down (50% of the 47-week advance), the market posted a higher low at $14.00 (July 1, 2010). The market continued to follow this time rhythm, showing turning points highlighted by projections of the 50% time retracement. The $16.25 low (November 29, 2010) came in 1 week before the 100% time projection, and the $21.45 high (May 31, 2011) came in 2 weeks after the 150% projection.

This application of 50% to time analysis is directly related to the study of cycles in market action. I explore cycles more in Chapter 8, "Beyond Trading Basics." The point of this exercise is to show how you can study Gann's most important mathematical relationships and apply them in ways that extend the examples he presented in his works.

Figure 5.3 illustrates the idea of looking at 50% within a consolidation formation. Distinct boundaries sometimes form as trading continues in a sideways range. Those boundaries can be parallel, converging (triangular), or diverging. Calculating the price retracements of the range, no matter what style boundary, yields a 50% value to watch where significant price action might develop.

Figure 5.4 shows a weekly chart of Alcatel Lucent. A period of sideways trading occurred after the $18.32 high was posted (March 8, 2004), with a lower boundary at $10.44 (July 7, 2005 low). Fifty percent of the $18.32/$10.44 range is 14.38, a level to monitor for significant price action. On July 3, 2007, the market posted a 3rd lower peak at $14.57, just 19 cents above the 50% retracement level before the market moved lower and eventually broke below the $10.44 boundary.

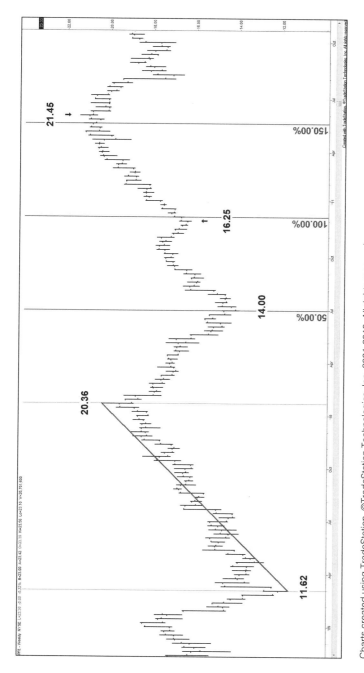

Figure 5.2 PFE, weekly, as of September 16, 2011

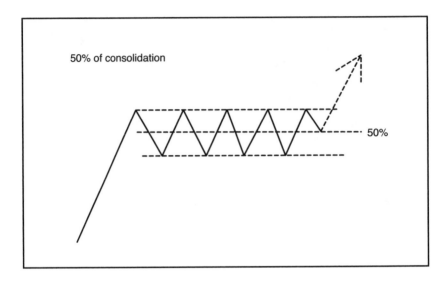

Figure 5.3 50% of consolidation

Figure 5.5 shows a series of price bars. The first pivot low represents a major reversal bar in a market. By "major," I mean an extreme
high or an extreme low level. Measuring the 50% retracement of just
that one bar yields a potential key area (in this case, support).

Figure 5.6 shows a weekly chart of Corn futures (July 2012). This
contract posted its extreme low at $3.93 1/4 (September 4, 2009). It
rallied to post a high at $4.80 (November 16/17, 2009) and then edged
lower. About 10 months after the extreme low was posted, corn fell to
$4.05 1/4 during the week of July 2, 2010. This low held 3 ticks above
the 50% value of the extreme pivot low range (bar high $4.16 1/4, bar
low $3.93 1/4, 50% at $4.04 3/4). This support held and became the
base low for the advance that ensued for the next 14 months.

Any Level of Eighth Retracement

Even though I've shown many examples focusing on the significance of the 50% retracement, remember that you should study and
observe all of Gann's favorite mathematical relationships to see how
they allow you to focus on pressure points in the market where significant time or price action might occur.

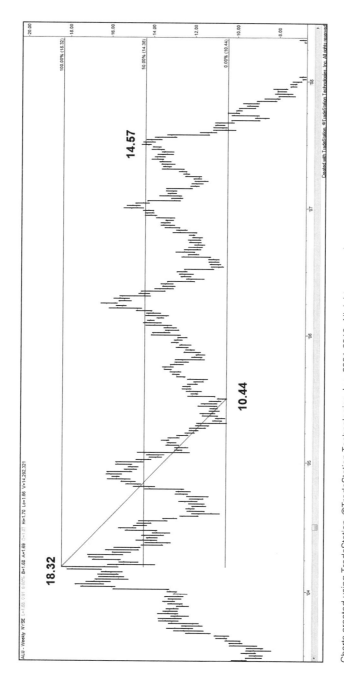

Charts created using TradeStation. ©TradeStation Technologies, Inc. 2001-2012. All rights reserved.

Figure 5.4 ALU, weekly, as of January 18, 2008

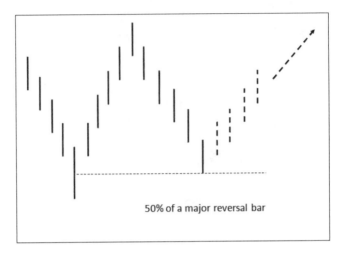

50% of a major reversal bar

Figure 5.5 50% of a major reversal

Figure 5.7 returns to the same Alcatel Lucent data that's in Figure 5.4, but this time, I've applied a full set of eighths retracements to the chart. You can see that the 50% retracement level was not the only one to prove significant in terms of price action. The $16.51 peak (April 5, 2006) tested the 75% retracement at 16.35. The $15.43 2nd lower peak (January 3, 2007) tested the 62.5% retracement at 15.37. The $11.41 higher low (March 23, 2007) tested the 12.5% retracement level at 11.43.

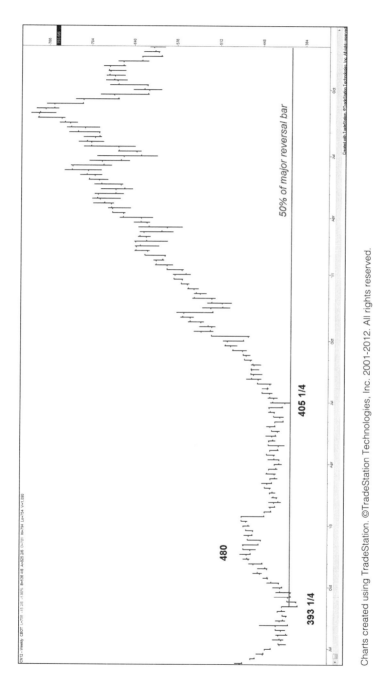

Figure 5.6 CN12, weekly, as of November 4, 2011

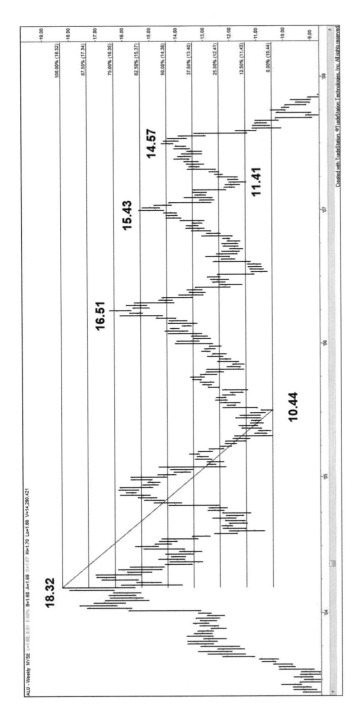

Figure 5.7 ALU, weekly, as of November 9, 2007

Gann's Principles Applied Outside of Price

All of the analysis I've presented thus far focuses on the basic elements of the chart: price, patterns, and time. However, there are many chart analysis tools that are enhanced when studied within the context of Gann's principles. I present a couple of the tools I have come to observe in this manner over time.

Trendlines

One of the most useful books I studied during my CMT exam preparations was *Technical Analysis of the Financial Markets,* by John J. Murphy (New York Institute of Finance, 1999). Although I was familiar with many of the basic technical analysis concepts presented in the text before I read it for the exams, I appreciated the approach that Murphy used to define and explain those concepts. I will reference some of his definitions for technical trading tools.

The first to address is the trendline. Murphy defines trendlines by directional movement.

> An up trendline is a straight line drawn upward to the right along successive reaction lows. A down trendline is drawn downward to the right along successive rally peaks.

Figures 5.8 and 5.9 illustrate these trendlines.

Murphy then goes on to say, "A tentative up trendline is first drawn under two successively higher lows, but needs a third test to confirm the validity of the trendline." Figure 5.10 illustrates this concept.

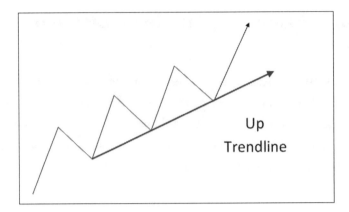

Figure 5.8 Up trendline

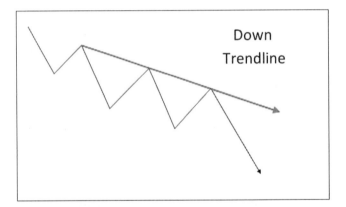

Figure 5.9 Down trendline

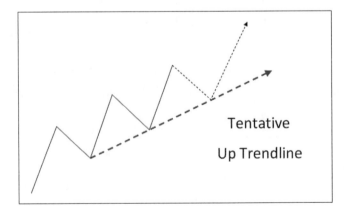

Figure 5.10 Tentative up trendline

I believe that any technical tool you add to your charts is of great value only if it (a) helps you trade with the trend or (b) helps you become aware of potential areas for trend reversal. One tenet that Gann stated more than once is that when the market has tested a level three times, it is more likely to break through that level than hold it a fourth time. So if that is the case, what are the limits of the traditional trendline, which contains three connecting points and measures their trend? I have observed that the trendline does not always provide secure trade entry points on its own. However, it does show a trader where the trend might *change*, at least in the short term.

Figure 5.11 shows a 15-minute chart of E-mini S&P 500 futures (September 2011 contract). After the market formed a low (anchor), the subsequent higher low (second point) provided the means to draw a tentative trendline. A subsequent higher low (third point) then confirmed the trendline as a rising support, according to the traditional definition. However, the next touch of the line, the fourth attempt, showed price breaking below the trendline.

Even though this example is of a 15-minute time frame, it can occur on any time frame. Let's take a look at another example, in which the breakdown occurred awhile after the trendline was confirmed.

Figure 5.12 shows a weekly chart of Google. After the market formed an anchor low at $437.00 (March 5, 2007), the subsequent higher low at $457.41 (May 15, 2007) provided the means to draw a tentative trendline. A subsequent higher low at $480.46 (August 16, 2007) then confirmed the trendline as a rising support by the traditional definition. You would then expect that a return to this line would hold as support.

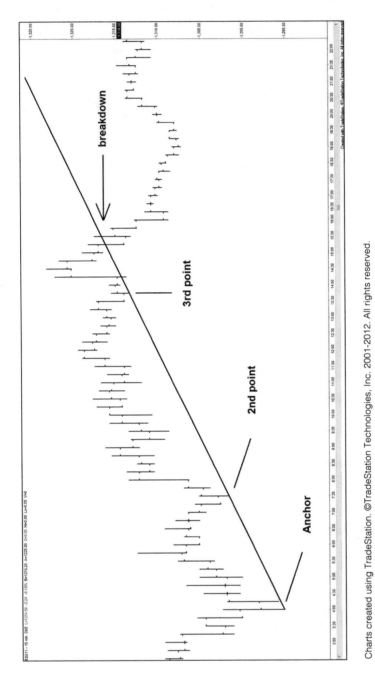

Charts created using TradeStation. ©TradeStation Technologies, Inc. 2001-2012. All rights reserved.

Figure 5.11 ESU11, 15 minute, as of July 12, 2011

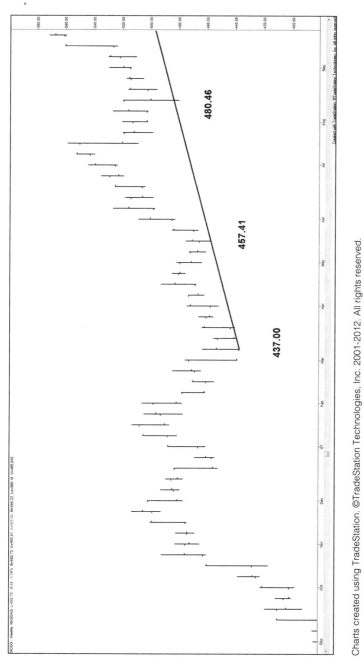

Charts created using TradeStation. ©TradeStation Technologies, Inc. 2001-2012. All rights reserved.

Figure 5.12 GOOG, weekly, as of September 28, 2007

However, moving forward several months on Figure 5.13, the market rallied to $747.24 (November 7, 2007) before turning lower. The next touch of the trendline, the fourth test, shows that the price broke below the trendline. Within a couple weeks, the former trendline reverted to resistance, as shown with the pivot high that formed at $541.04 (February 14, 2008). A couple months later, the former trendline became an approximate center axis for a zone of consolidation that ultimately formed a lower swing high at $602.45 (May 2, 2008).

Even though this is a chart of weekly price action, similar movement can and does occur on all time frames. The examples presented are intended to guide you to make practical use of trendlines in your analysis, not to just follow them blindly.

Another way to use trendlines toward greater analytical prowess is to revisit the key elements that comprise a trendline. By the traditional definition, two highs (or lows) create a tentative trendline, and a third high (or low) confirms the trendline. However, what would happen if we used the *range* of the high or low to create a pair of trendlines?

Figure 5.14 shows a daily chart of Google. A rising trendline originating from the $433.63 low (July 1, 2010) connected to the $473.02 low (June 24, 2011) and was confirmed on October 4, 2011, posting a low at $480.60. However, if one had projected a parallel of the tentative trendline from the high of the July 1st origination bar (high value is $448.40), the trendline channel would have alerted the trader when the $490.86 low (August 19, 2011) came in.

Figure 5.15 also shows a daily chart of Google. The decline trendline off the $642.96 peak (January 19, 2011) that joined the $641.73 high (January 21, 2011) and was confirmed by the $631.18 high (February 18, 2011). If a projected parallel of the trendline had been drawn off the low value of the January 19 origination bar (low value is $629.66), the trader would have been alerted to the formation of the $595.19 swing high near the projected line (April 1, 2011).

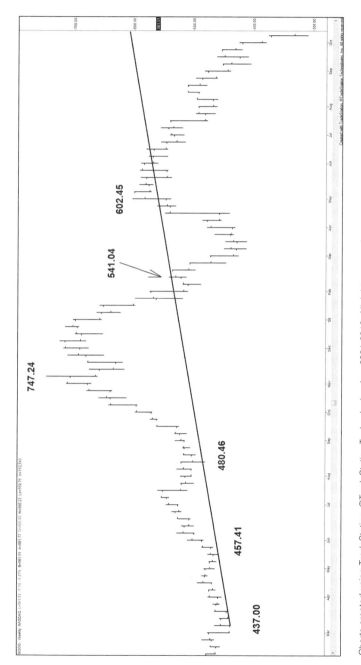

Charts created using TradeStation. ©TradeStation Technologies, Inc. 2001-2012. All rights reserved.

Figure 5.13 GOOG, weekly, as of October 10, 2008

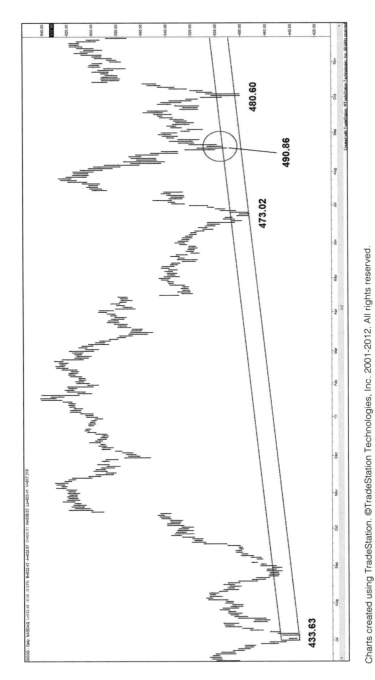

Figure 5.14 GOOG, daily, as of November 21, 2011

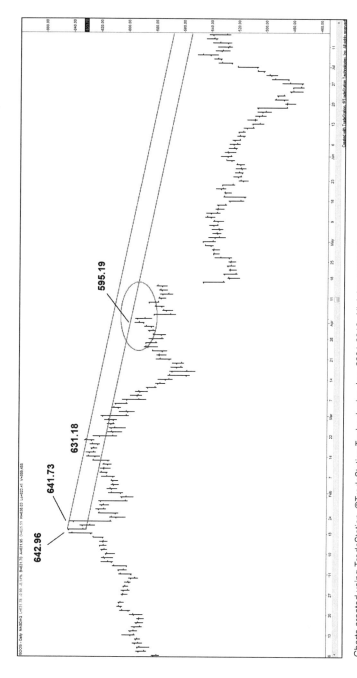

Figure 5.15 GOOG, daily, as of July 14, 2011

Oscillators

Many traders and investors who use technical analysis methods to make their buy/sell decisions use indicators derived from price action as part of their trading plans. One category of indicators is that of oscillators. An oscillator is a price-derived indicator that fluctuates between 0 and 100. The Relative Strength Index (RSI) is a commonly used oscillator. When the RSI crosses above 70, the security is considered overbought, indicating that buying power is waning. When the RSI is below 30, the security is considered oversold, indicating that selling power is losing force.

Although oscillators may be applied to a chart and observed for signals during trending as well as nontrending markets, the key to using oscillators effectively is to use them differently during each of these trend scenarios. The value of oscillators is in being able to discern extreme areas in a market. So when the market is trending, the movement of the oscillators can point to the likely continuation or reversal of the trend. During nontrending market times, the oscillators can help point out the best entries and exits for short-term trades within a consolidation range, accumulation phase, or distribution phase.

So why am I talking about oscillators when Gann never did? Because if oscillators are price derived, and Gann uncovered clear tradable patterns that occur in price movement, isn't it possible that such patterns can also reveal themselves within the oscillators? Let's take a look and find out.

Figure 5.16 depicts the May 2012 contract of Sugar futures. The RSI made three sections down from the 80.48 value (July 12, 2011). The thin horizontal line drawn out from the 62.66 value (October 14, 2011) toward the 61.83 value (January 23, 2012) highlights the fact that the rally from the 22.53 low value (November 25, 2011) retraced nearly all the RSI move from 62.66 to 22.53. More significantly, the period of time of the rally from 22.43 to 61.83 exceeded the last rally before extreme lows were reached. This movement compares directly to the previously described Gann Buying Point #5!

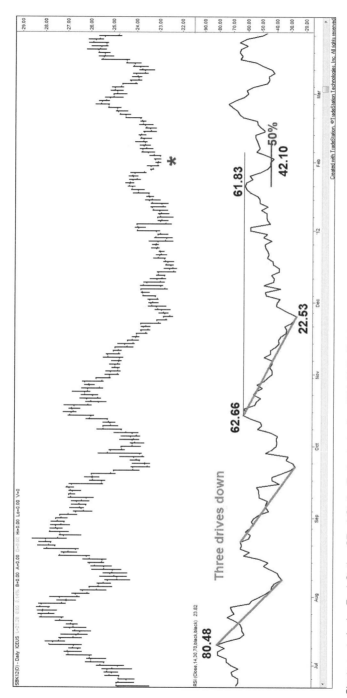

Charts created using TradeStation. ©TradeStation Technologies, Inc. 2001-2012. All rights reserved.

Figure 5.16 SBK12, daily, as of March 23, 2012

The rest of that buying point description says, "If the last rally was 3 or 4 weeks, when the advance from the bottom is more than 3 or 4 weeks, consider that the trend has turned up and commodities are a safer buy on a secondary reaction." This can be directly compared back to the behavior of the RSI in Figure 5.14. The RSI fell from 61.83 to 42.10 (February 2, 2012), testing 43.96, the 50% retracement of the 22.43/61.83 section up. Therefore, the price pivot low marked with an asterisk indicates a buy zone that is reinforced by the Gann signals present within the RSI.

Another commonly used oscillator is Williams %R. As with the RSI, the Williams %R oscillator moves between 0 and 100. When Williams %R is over 80, the security is considered overbought. When the Williams %R is below 30, the security is considered oversold.

Figure 5.17 depicts Pitney Bowes. The Williams %R made three sections up from 3.67 (week of August 13, 2010 value) to 99.31 (week of December 17, 2010 value). The thin horizontal line drawn out from the 74.02 value (week of November 26, 2010) toward the 71.94 value (week of January 7, 2011) highlights the fact that the decline from the 99.31 value broke below the 74.02 value. This move had broken the bottom of the last reaction, turning trend down. This movement compares directly to the previously described Gann Selling Point #3!

The earlier part of that selling point description starts with, "Sell on a *secondary rally* after ...." Comparing this description directly to the behavior of the Williams %R in this example, the secondary rally came in at 98.26 (week of February 11, 2011 value).

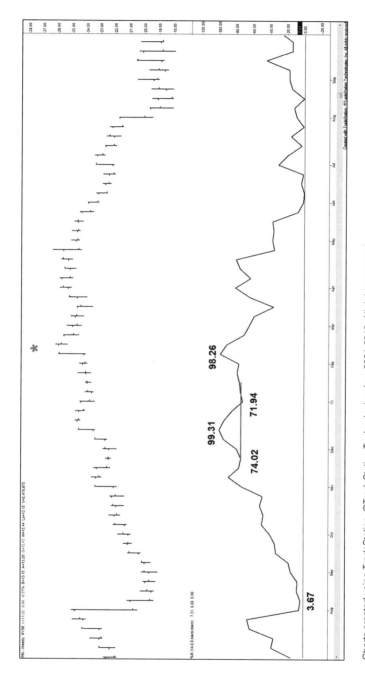

Charts created using TradeStation. ©TradeStation Technologies, Inc. 2001-2012. All rights reserved.

Figure 5.17 PBI, weekly, as of September 30, 2011

The price pivot high marked with an asterisk indicates a sell zone marked by the Gann signals present within the Williams %R. However, remember that *price is king* is paramount, and applications of Gann analysis to oscillators is of only secondary importance. In this scenario, the bearish action of the Williams %R would have cautioned longs to tighten their stops, but the oscillator behavior is not meant to be used as a call to trade action all on its own. It would come into play several bars later, when price would fail to post higher highs on a closing basis, and the Williams %R action would reinforce a subsequent short position.

The Importance of the Closing Price

After first studying Gann's buying and selling points as delineated in the *Commodities* book, I began to observe the market to practice identifying these signals. However, I often found that I looked at the overall OHLC bar action and did not understand why a certain signal played out the way that it did. Over time, I observed the following: A *test* of a key support or resistance in the market, but a *failure* of the subsequent price bars to post a close decisively through that level, often led to a change in the expected price action.

Figure 5.18 depicts the weekly price action of Bank of America.

Figure 5.19 zooms in toward the top half of the price action, where a higher high was posted at $18.64 on October 14, 2009. About six months later, the market rallied to test that level during the week of April 9, 2010. The next week saw trading reach as high as $19.86 (April 15, 2010), but the week closed at $18.05, a price level below $18.64. The week following the $19.86 high saw trading reach $18.91, but again the closing price failed to surpass $18.64; this time, it fell to $17.87. Lower highs and lower lows followed suit.

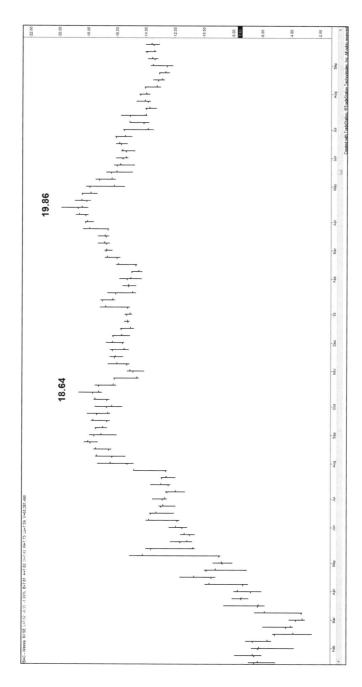

Charts created using TradeStation. ©TradeStation Technologies, Inc. 2001-2012. All rights reserved.

Figure 5.18 BAC, weekly, as of October 29, 2010

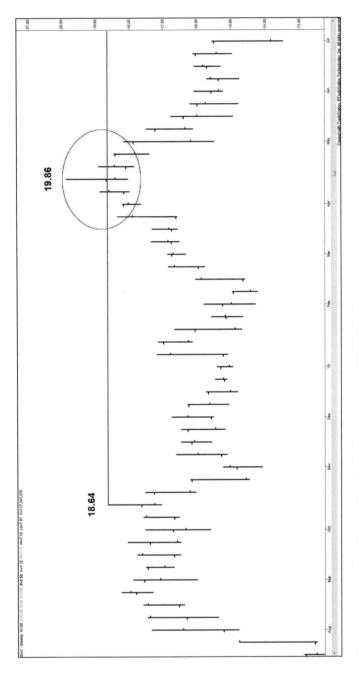

Figure 5.19 BAC, weekly, as of July 9, 2010

These probes above $18.64 but a failure to sustain a breakthrough on a closing basis illustrate the concept of the test failure, which my father taught me. This particular example is of a bearish test failure because a drop in prices followed.

Moving to a daily chart, Figure 5.20 shows that the market posted a steady decline from the $19.86 peak.

Using Figure 5.21 to highlight the bottom of the chart, you can see that a lower low was posted at $11.03 on October 26, 2010. About a month later, the market declined to test that level, on November 30, 2010. The OHLC bar reached a low of $10.91 before closing at $10.95, which should have indicated that the downside momentum would continue. However, the next bar on November 31 posted a close at $11.29, back above the key $11.03 level. Higher highs and higher lows followed suit. This illustrates an example of a bullish test failure because a low was tested and a rise in prices followed.

As you can see, a two-bar window follows the initial level test in which the test failure might form. However, this is not a signal that is meant to be targeted for market entry. Its value is in letting you know when a buying or selling point is *not* playing out as expected. The importance of knowing when a signal is not working is that it allows you to exit the trade efficiently, protecting as much profit as possible or minimizing losses. Chapter 6, "Trade and Capital Management," further explains the methods Gann recommended for maximizing profits and cutting losses.

Recognizing test failures is one way closing prices can enhance your analysis, but others also exist.

As Chapter 1, "The Work of W.D. Gann," explained, using simple OHLC charts is the best format to help you start your study of Gann's trading methods, since they show patterns relatively clearly. However, what happens when you are looking at an OHLC chart of a security, whether it's a 5-minute chart or a daily chart, and you find yourself struggling to see the sections the market has formed and where the true high and low points exist?

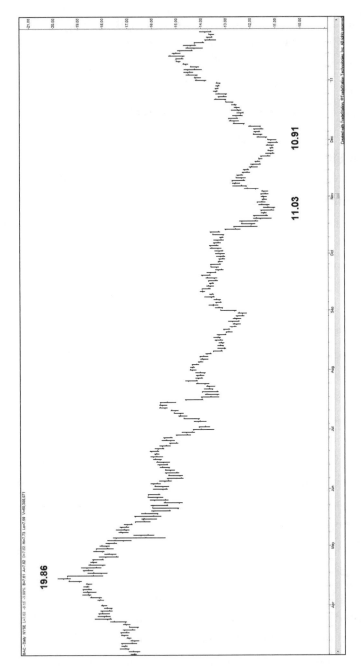

Figure 5.20 BAC, daily, as of January 25, 2011

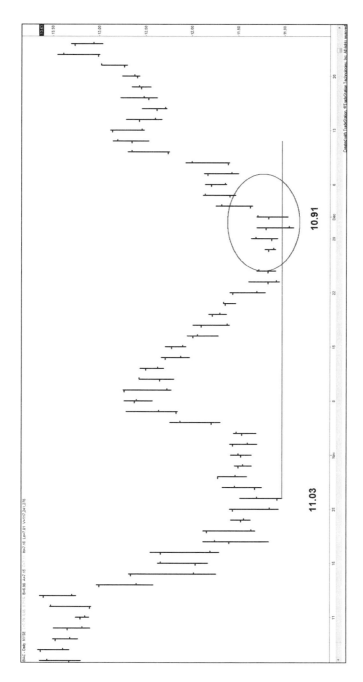

Charts created using TradeStation. ©TradeStation Technologies, Inc. 2001-2012. All rights reserved.

Figure 5.21 BAC, daily, as of December 27, 2010

Figure 5.22 of the Gold Cash Index shows the weekly chart peaking at $232.72 (December 7, 2010). A lower pivot high formed at $230.48 (April 8, 2011) before the index continued lower. The subsequent price action is a bit volatile when comparing the swing sizes to those of the previous advance from $144.55 (February 5, 2010).

To get a clear sense of how the uptrend ended and what exactly is going on within the volatile swings, it helps to look at a simpler version of the chart. Generally, simplifying a situation involves removing elements of information from it, and the process is no different here. Instead of studying this chart with the open, high, low, and close of every period (week) shown, convert the image to a line chart. This allows you to focus on one aspect of each trading session—the open, the high, the low, or the close. The close is desired as the input for a line chart because, at the end of a trading session, the closing price represents the agreement that the buyers and sellers have reached regarding the value of that entity for that session. The opening of the next session, in many cases (especially with shorter-term charts), most often is at or near the closing price of the previous session. Viewing a line chart showing close price only often clears up any confusion about what sections are present.

Figure 5.23 shows the close-only version of the Gold Cash Index chart. The high and low points are now labeled in italics because they indicate the closing highs and closing lows of their relevant time periods. The italics differentiate these values from the actual highs and lows reached, as in Figure 5.22.

Based on the line chart, the highest close for the index during the time observed was at $228.95 (April 8, 2011). The market made three sections lower to reach $190.12 (June, 17, 2011 close), breaking below the higher low at $199.71 (January 28, 2011 close). The index then corrected higher in two moves, reaching $223.21 (September 9, 2011 close). The weakness from this area occurred in predominantly two-section structures. All of this was easily derived by simply converting an OHLC chart to a line chart based on closing price values.

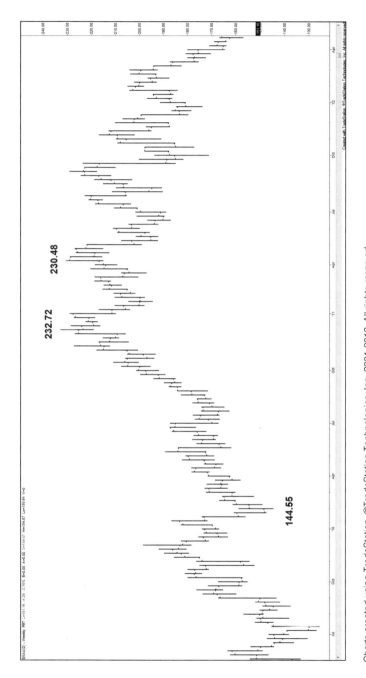

Charts created using TradeStation. ©TradeStation Technologies, Inc. 2001-2012. All rights reserved.

Figure 5.22 $XAU, weekly, as of April 26, 2012

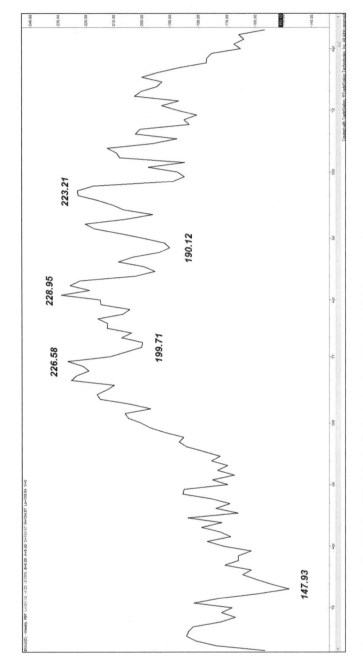

Figure 5.23 $XAU, weekly, as of April 26, 2012

The importance of the closing price is not only in seeing market sections more clearly, but also in providing additional anchor points for drawing retracements such as Gann eighths. If the low price of a swing low and the high price of a swing high are good anchors for retracements, calculating retracements of the closing price of a swing low and the closing price of a swing high can help focus on the true range of market action. The lowest low at which a market closed and the highest high at which a market closed over a given period of time show the true area where supply and demand reside. Again, this is because the closing price of any period is where the buyers and sellers agreed on the value of the security. Drawing retracements from the lowest close to the highest close, therefore, enables you as a trader to focus on the bulk of the action.

Figure 5.24 uses the same Gold Cash Index data as the previous figures, but I've added more information to the chart by showing trading from the swing low preceding the full advance up to the December 2010 high.

The $70.86 close (October 24, 2008) marks the low anchor for the eighths retracements. The $228.95 close marks the high anchor. Drawing the retracements off the extreme close levels captures the bulk of the move and keeps you focused on the zones of support and resistance present. Too often, we get caught up in a need for a market to rally or decline precisely to retracements we have drawn out, but we hardly ever think about what goes into choosing the anchors for those retracements. The most obvious benefit of drawing retracements anchored on closing levels is seen with the price action at point (A). That high was posted on September 8, 2011, and reached $228.98, pushing only 3 cents above the resistance at 228.95, a sign of the validity of that 228.95 as a resistance level.

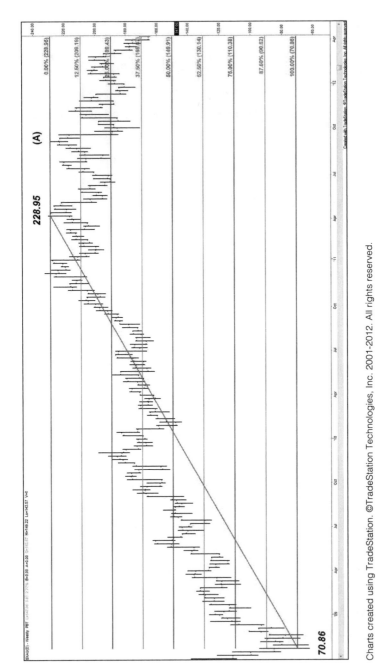

Charts created using TradeStation. ©TradeStation Technologies, Inc. 2001-2012. All rights reserved.

Figure 5.24 $XAU, weekly, as of April 26, 2012

6

Trade and Capital Management

The loss of capital is the number one reason traders/investors stop participating in the market. Therefore, preserving one's capital is of utmost importance.

Gann presented capital management rules both directly and indirectly throughout his works. I boil down the basics of what he presented, to get you started on the right foot toward Gann's money-management style.

Let's return to the phases of a trade, as presented earlier in Chapter 4, "Trading the Market":

1. Trend assessment
2. Signal observation
3. Risk assessment
4. Order placement
5. Trade initiation
6. Trade management
7. Trade exit
8. Review

These phases form a continuous loop. We've covered trend assessment and signal observation. Now we explore the remaining phases.

Risk Assessment

In this third phase of a trade, the trader looks at the amount of working capital in the account, to construct his trade to manage potential risk. No matter how large or small the amount of capital, Gann's basic tenets (expressed in more than one of his books) provide ways to manage the capital as each trade opportunity arises.

> **Gann Rule (Affirmative) #1:** Divide your capital into ten equal parts and always risk less than one-tenth of your capital on any one trade.

Now, anyone with trade experience reading the statement above will likely find a trade risking 10% of one's capital to be too high relative to the account size. I agree with this notion, and I have yet to meet anyone who in fact risks 10% of his capital on one trade. The main point to glean from the rule as stated is as follows: According to the situation described, if the first trade becomes a loss, then the trader would have to be wrong the next nine times in a row to blow out his account. Gann shared that this is extremely unlikely based on the buying and selling tenets that he presented. Therefore, what's important to understand here is that the less you risk on any one trade, the greater chance you have of preserving your capital in the long haul. It is up to the individual trader to define the risk per trade, as a percentage or fixed dollar amount, within the confines of the 10%.

Based on a starting account size of $10,000, the capital would divide into ten equal parts of $1,000 each. For the examples ahead, I will employ a 2% maximum risk per trade. For a $10,000 account, that would be $200.

If the first trade is a winner, the account size obviously increases, but your risk per trade should not increase at that point. The time to adjust the maximum risk capital is when the account has doubled in size. This means that funds are not to be withdrawn after one or many winning trades. The goal is to make profits on an unchanging initial capital amount and then to remove the profits from the account in a systematic fashion.

> **Gann Rule (Affirmative) #11:** Accumulate a surplus. After you have made a series of successful trades, put some money into a surplus account to be used as an emergency fund.

The goal per Gann's money-management advice is to make your initial capital work for you.

- When the account doubles to $20,000, remove $5,000 (half the profits) from the account to put into an emergency (or savings) fund.
- Leave the remaining $5,000 (other half of profits) in the trading account. You now have a total of $15,000 in the trading account.
- Continuing with the 2% risk maximum per trade, the new maximum risk amount per trade would be $300.

On the other hand, if your account is not profitable (you are losing more capital than you are making), the time to adjust your risk management is when you suffer three losses in a row. You make the adjustments based on your remaining capital.

> **Gann Rule (Affirmative) #3:** Always trade lot sizes and amounts of risk that fit within the limits of your capital.

Given the guidelines based on a $10,000 account, the minimum capital remaining after three losses in a row would be $9,400, the difference of the initial account balance and the $600 ($200 × 3) lost on the trades.

- So if you have three losses in a row, risk only 2% of the *remaining* capital. Using the $9,400 minimum as a model, the new maximum risk per trade would equal $188.

Now, if the account continues to lose, and at some point suffers three losses again, you would take additional steps to decrease your initial risk. Based on the $9,400 new account size, the minimum capital remaining after another three losses in a row would be $8,836, the difference of the initial account balance and the $564 ($188× 3) lost on the trades.

- If three losses occur in a row again, risk only 2% of the remaining minimum $8,836 capital.

- Using the $8,836 minimum as a model, the new maximum risk per trade would equal $176.72.

Gann talks about the trading unit as the number of units (shares, contracts, and so on) of a security involved in one trade. For beginning money management, that does not need to be addressed separately because the trading unit or lot size directly relates to the rules stated previously. Therefore, if rows of losses occur as described, the number of units traded will decrease in line with the decrease in the maximum risk per trade.

Gann Rule (Affirmative) #8: Distribute risk equally among traded markets. Risk only up to 10% of your capital in any one market.

As you trade a market and get filled on a position, you might encounter more opportunities to trade the prevailing trend. However, your total risk in any market, no matter how many opportunities to add on arise, should always total less than 10% of your capital. If you see a valid trade signal in another market while you are active in one, you can invest in that second market as well. The key is to not put all your eggs in one basket. Keeping your trades diversified and low risk will make capital preservation much easier.

Placement of Orders

Gann Rule (Affirmative) #14: Enter and exit the market only on definite signals, with emotions in check.

When I first started trading, I found it difficult to set up my trades. I would see the signal, but the three components of the strategy—the entry, the objective, and the protective stop—would not easily pop into my head. So my father suggested the following: When you see a clear signal that tells you to buy or sell the market you are observing, first ask yourself, "Where would I put the stop?" If you do that, the rest of the trade will fall into place.

I implemented this way of thinking early on, and I have followed this advice since. Now I can't even imagine placing a trade strategy without *first* calculating where the protective stop would be.

Gann Rule (Affirmative) #2: Use stop loss orders. Always protect a trade when you make it (on commodities) with a stop loss order 1 to 3 cents (up to 5 cents) away—for cotton, 20 to 40 points (up to 60 points) away; for stocks, 3 to 5 points away.

Although the cents and points in this rule were derived from the way markets moved during Gann's time, they are still useful guides. Ultimately, place your stop so that you are risking less than your predetermined amount of capital (2% is the example used) on any one trade.

Gann Rule (Affirmative) #16: After you've placed a stop loss order, always keep it, and move it only in the direction that minimizes risk/protects profits.

Since I placed my first paper trade, I have determined the price level to place the protective stop loss order on a position, whether I was scalping or trend trading, and whether I was buying or selling. This is because Gann's works, the base of my trading education, focus on the placement of the stop, not the determination of the objective.

Along with the rules shared in Chapter 4, for example, Gann added reminders about how to manage trades. Included in the description for the listed Gann Buying Point #8, he wrote, "Always use STOP LOSS ORDERS for protection in case the market reverses. REMEMBER, YOU CAN'T BE RIGHT ALL THE TIME. The STOP LOSS ORDER gets you out if you are wrong. Try to take small losses and large profits. That is the way to keep ahead of the market."

The value of everything Gann had to say about protecting your trades cannot be overstated.

To determine the placement of the protective stop loss order, you have a few options, as described in the buying and selling points.

- Above swing highs/below swing lows
- Above price bar highs/below price bar lows

Different ways to assess the stop also exist. A money stop is based on an allotted risk amount. For example, based on the $10,000 starting capital model, a money stop placed on a long position would not necessarily relate to any actual market movement. It would directly relate only to the maximum loss per trade of $200, based on an estimated entry price.

A logical stop, however, takes into account the price action surrounding the entry point. I prefer the use of logical stops because, if they are triggered, they are often clearly telling you that your position in the market was wrong in relation to the trend. However, remember that, when using logical stops, you must take action on a trade only if the placement of the logical stop still fits within your maximum risk parameters. *No trade is worth making* if it breaks your money-management rules. It will be impossible to consistently preserve your capital if you make exceptions to your money-management rules.

Per the capital-management guidelines explored earlier, traders often come to think of the maximum risk per trade as a goal to reach. Whether they decide that they should risk a maximum of 1%, 2%, or 5% per trade, they sometimes seek it out—even when risking that much is not necessary to be able to take advantage of the trade set up. Instead, traders should look to minimize risk for maximum rewards. For example, situations might arise in which a logical stop fits your maximum risk parameters and even leaves room for you to increase your lot size within those parameters. In these situations, do not attempt to increase your lot size simply because you have room to do so. Take the lowest-risk trades that fit your trading plan/signals/ parameters. That is where you will reap the greatest reward.

The real key to placing useful stops is to study the market or markets you trade and observe the following: When the marked rallied to prior bottoms while in a downtrend and then resumed lower, by how much (if at all) did the market move above that old bottom? Similarly, when the market corrected to former tops while in an uptrend and then resumed higher, by how much (if at all) did that market move below that old top? Knowing this helps you know how much the market of your choice tests key levels and allows you to place the most effective stops.

For example, when trading E-mini S&P 500 futures on an intraday basis, I use margins of at least two tick[1] movements as the starting point for my stop placement. Why two ticks or more? In my observation, I have noticed that when there is a false break of a high or low, or a "failure," it is most often only by one tick before the prior trend resumes. Therefore, giving the trade some breathing room prevents some of the situations in which false alarms of direction change trigger stops. Also, by allowing a failure to play out and still be in the trade, I have time to get at out or near breakeven and reassess the situation.

---

[1] A tick is the minimum fluctuation within the market. In the E-mini S&P 500 futures market, this value is one fourth of a point (.25), equal to $12.50.

If the market is entering a consolidation phase, it will become evident sooner rather than later. If the market did change trend, I've minimized my loss upon realizing the change of scenario. However, if the market does resume the trend and my trade *would have* been profitable, I can re-enter on a clear signal instead of staying in the trade because of hope. As Gann wrote, "Trading on hope or fear will never help you to make a success."[2]

Trade Initiation

> **Gann Rule (Affirmative) #9:** Let the market show you at what price to enter a buy or a sell.

Where to enter a market after recognizing a signal and assessing a stop level ultimately relates to capital preservation, just like everything else in trade management. However, in the original version of rule #9, Gann advised to sell at market. Perhaps he meant that literally, as in only using market orders in which the trade would be filled at the current market price. But I believe that what he really meant was to pay attention to what the market is telling you about where to enter after a clear signal forms.

I believe this because of the way prices fluctuate. They expand and contract directly in line with traders' emotions, which are connected to a multitude of sources, including market fundamentals. Therefore, fixating on a certain price target to enter the market long or short will not help you make as much money as if you focus on where on the price scale the signal is occurring and adjust your entrance plan accordingly.

---

[2] W.D. Gann, *How to Make Profits Trading in Commodities* (Pomeroy, WA: Lambert-Gann, 2009), 6.

Management of Trade

> **Gann Rule (Affirmative) #6:** Enter the market and stay in a trade only as long as you are sure of the market indications according to your rules.
>
> **Gann Rule (Affirmative) #23:** Change your position in the market only with a good reason. When you make a trade, let it be for some good reason or according to some definite rule; then stay in the trade until you have a definite indication of a change in trend.

Sometimes when you read what Gann advises, it sounds like a broken record. This is because he wants to drill concepts into your head. These two rules exemplify that.

However, after you have entered a trade, you might decide to add more contracts or shares to your position as the market moves favorably. This is called pyramiding.

> **Gann Rule (Affirmative) #21:** Select the commodities that show strong uptrend to pyramid on the buying side and the ones that show definite downtrend to sell short.
>
> **Gann Rule (Affirmative) #13:** Pyramid only on trades that are showing profit. This is how you can make the most profits on sustained moves.
>
> **Gann Rule (Affirmative) #20:** Pyramid at the right time. On a long position, wait until the security is very active and has crossed Resistance Levels before buying more. On a short position, wait until the security has broken out of the zone of distribution before selling more.

In Chapter 7, "Bringing It All Together," I share an example of a trade that Gann walked through in his *Commodities* book. It clearly illustrates how he advised to pyramid.

Whether or not you pyramid on a trade, if it is moving favorably, you will want to protect your accumulated profits.

Gann Rule (Affirmative) #4: Always protect your accumulated profit. On a long position, raise your stop loss order once your profit equals your initial risk. On a short position, lower your stop loss order once your profit equals your initial risk.

Rule #4 couldn't be clearer. To use it in an example, if you bought 100 shares of stock at a price of $5.00 with a protective stop order at $4.00, your maximum risk of loss would be $100 (100 × $1.00). If the market moves favorably and advances to $6.00, you would have an accumulated profit of $100 and would therefore raise your protective stop to the original $5.00 entry point, at the minimum. If you wanted to cover the cost of commissions or lock in some profit, you could raise the stop loss even higher. But the key is to eliminate the chance of loss as soon as the market presents the opportunity to do so. Again, this makes capital preservation much easier to achieve.

When a stop has moved to breakeven, how do you manage it from there, assuming that the market is continuing favorably (you're making money on the trade)? One option is to use retracements.

Yes, retracements. They don't have to be limited to entering and exiting trades based on major signals. They can also be used to manage a trade while it's live. Retracements can provide clear levels for placement of initial protective stop loss orders as well as trailing stops.

Figure 6.1 illustrates a wide-range band of trading with distinct upper and lower boundaries. A short trade initiated near the upper resistance, and the market reversed lower to hold the range. Instead of focusing on the one- or two-bar highs within a consolidation pattern for trailing stops, draw a fourths retracement (break the range into four equal parts) creating new levels to use for adjusting trail stops. If the market reached the first retracement level, the stop would lower to breakeven (price where the short was entered). If the halfway point (two-fourths) was met, the stop would lower to just above the previously met one-fourth retracement. If the three-fourths level were met, in terms of accumulated profit, the stop would move to just above the halfway point. This provides a clear way to trail stops, as opposed to the traditional Gann method of two-bar highs or lower swings. Basically, don't be afraid to apply analysis concepts to the different phases of a trade.

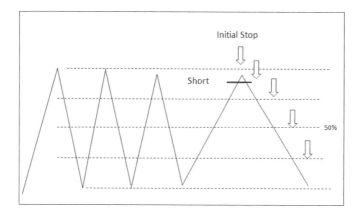

Figure 6.1 Using retracements for protective stop placement

Another way to manage a trade that is going favorably is to move the protective stop order along bar highs or lows. Gann talks about runaway trends, the steep price action that occurs during the last sections of bull or bear markets. These are of great importance, and Gann emphasizes that they are the moves in which most great traders' profit is made. When the market picks up momentum in an uptrend, each session tends to open higher within the range of the preceding bar and rarely even touches the low of the previous bar. If a correction appears and extends over the period of two bars or more, it may break the low of one previous bar before the uptrend resumes. This type of move often affects inexperienced traders the most because they find the one-bar break to be a sign of trend change and exit their longs— or, worse, go short. The runaway move instead continues higher after the correction that took out the low of only the one most recent bar. Figure 6.2 illustrates this type of price action.

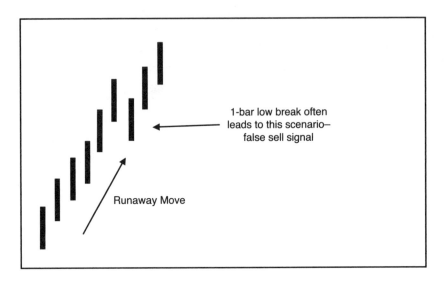

1-bar low break often
leads to this scenario–
false sell signal

Runaway Move

Figure 6.2 1-bar low break in a runaway move

Ultimately, the runaway move will cap out for a high or consolidation, but how does one maximize the profit on the long position before this happens? *By watching for the break of the two bars preceding the current one.* When the market makes a correction, taking out the two previously established bars lows, it becomes the first warning of impending trend change. That is the time to tighten stops, or to exit on the market's next attempt at a move higher. Figure 6.3 illustrates the described price action.

Even using the two-bar rule for stop placement is reasonable, and I have implemented that as a trailing stop methodology in runaway moves, even down to a 1-minute chart. The key to obtaining trading success with this information is to get a sense of how each particular market moves. Take a look at Figures 6.4 and 6.5, illustrating soybean futures (July 2012 contract).

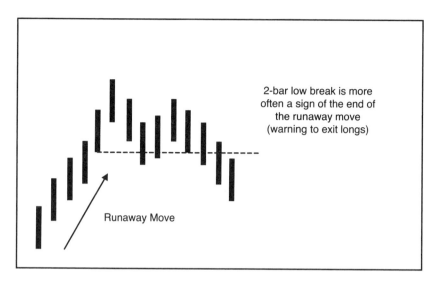

Figure 6.3 2-bar low break in a runaway move

Figure 6.5 zooms in on the up move from $12.33 (February 10, 2012 low) to $13.43 1/2 (March 5, 2012 high). Placing a 3-cent trailing stop based on one-bar lows would have exited longs at $13.27 1/4, on the break of the $13.30 1/4 low (March 5, 2012).

However, applying a two-bar trailing stop method, Figure 6.6 shows that any long position would have been held longer. The minor correction from $13.43 1/2 saw one bar post a lower high and lower low before the uptrend resumed. Because that second bar had a lower high, indicating only a reaction, the trailing stop stayed in position, at $13.20 (3 cents below the low of the bar preceding the $13.43 1/2 price bar). However, later when the market reached $13.83 1/2 on March 16, the next day's bar posted a *higher* high at $13.84 1/2, as well as a lower low, indicating a reversal. This then made the March 16 and March 17 bars the reference for the trailing stop, and the stop was moved up to $13.66 1/2 (3 cents below the low of the $13.84 1/2 price bar). On March 20, the market continued lower and the trailing stop was triggered. The diagonal blue line shows the additional profit captured by using a two-bar trailing stop method instead of a one-bar trailing stop method.

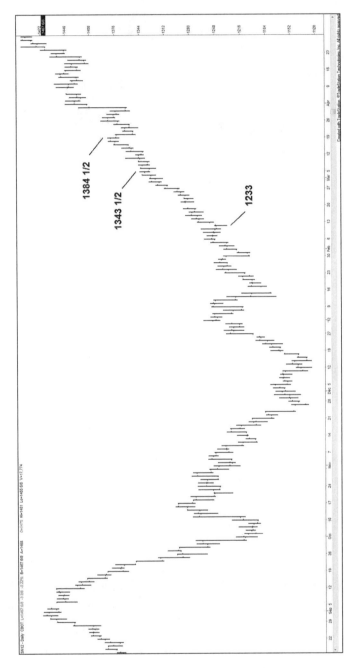

Figure 6.4 SN12, daily, as of May 1, 2012

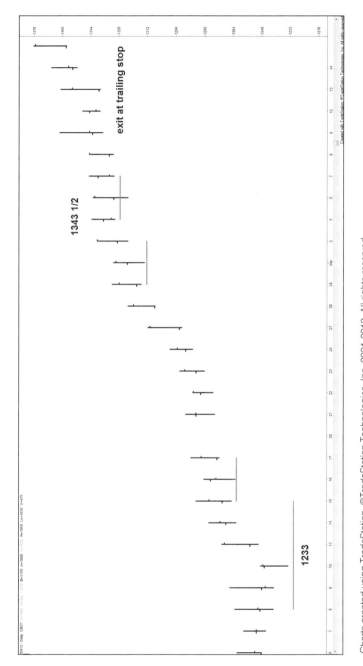

Charts created using TradeStation. ©TradeStation Technologies, Inc. 2001-2012. All rights reserved.

Figure 6.5 SN12, daily, as of March 14, 2012

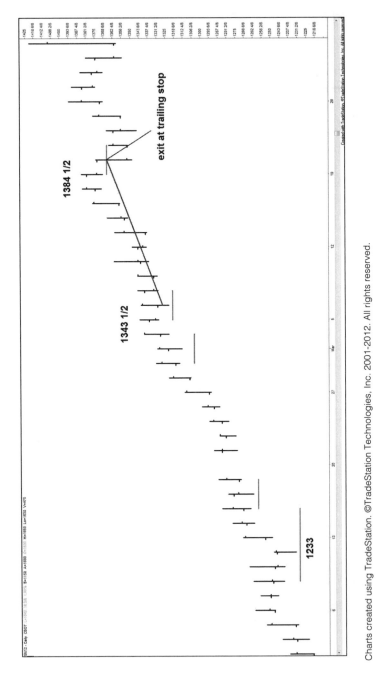

Figure 6.6 SN12, daily, as of March 30, 2012

Notice that I did not talk about where a long might have been entered. That is because I want to keep your focus on the movement of the trailing stops. It doesn't matter where a long might have been entered after the $12.33 low was posted—what's important is that you see how the way you manage the trade has a direct effect on how much profit you can pull from it.

Overall, your management of a trade should adjust to the market's current character:

In a sideways market range, take most of your profits (more than half) at the first objective. Do not hope for a breakout; instead, let the market show that it is breaking out of the sideways range.

In a creeping (slow-moving) market, you can trail stops according to each higher swing for longs or lower swing for shorts. Or you can utilize the autostop features of your trading software to help lock in most of the profit (one-half to two-thirds) of the current potential profit for the move. In a slow-moving market, you should be giving back only a small portion of your net profits if the trailing stop is triggered.

In a runaway or steep market, you can use the *bar* lows/highs on the selected time frame to keep you with the trend. Remember the two-bar rule. This will keep you in the trade for the majority of the move.

Trade Exit

Gann Rule (Affirmative) #10: Close your trade only with a good reason. Follow up with a stop loss order to protect your profits.

Gann Rule (Affirmative) #28: Focus on getting in the market according to your rules and out of the market according to your rules.

The same buying and selling points (among other methods) that you use to enter the market are the same tools that you can use to exit the market.

> **Gann Rule (Affirmative) #22:** If you have a position on and the market starts to move against it, get out at the market, take your loss, and wait for another opportunity. Or rely on your stop order to minimize your losses.

Ultimately, you have five ways to exit a trade that respect the rules.

1. An adjusted protective stop is triggered after the market has moved favorably, exiting the trade at breakeven (no loss, no profit).
2. A trailing stop is triggered, locking in profit.
3. The market reaches a predetermined objective and an exit order is triggered at that price, locking in profit.
4. The market goes against the trade and the original protective stop is triggered, taking a loss.
5. The market goes against the trade and you realize that you no longer have indications to stay in, so you exit at market, taking a loss.

Review

Reviewing each trade is extremely important, whether it resulted in a profit or a loss.

The first aspect to review reverts back to rule #28. Ask yourself whether you got in the market according to your rules and you got out of the market according to your rules.

If the trade was profitable ...

Gann Rule (Affirmative) #24: Maintain your lot size and maximum risk amount after a long period of success or a period of profitable trades. (Increase your lot size and maximum risk amount only after you have doubled your capital and added back half to your initial account size, increasing your total tradable capital amount.)

If the trade resulted in a loss ...

Gann Rule (Affirmative) #27: If your lot size contains multiple contracts, reduce the number of contracts traded after the first loss.

Overall ...

Gann Rule (Affirmative) #15: Take large profits and small losses.

Did you protect as much profit as reasonably possible, according to your rules? If the trade was a loss, did you minimize the loss, according to your rules?

After you have reviewed the trade at least once, you can return your focus to the market. Sometimes when you've exited a trade at the end of a strong move, you quickly see opportunities which form to enter the market in the opposite direction (new trend). Make sure that if you recognize such a signal, you consider taking it only if it fits your predetermined risk/reward parameters.

Similarly, you might have exited a trade when the market moved against it and you realized you were on the wrong side of the move. After you have reviewed your trade, you can revisit the chart to see if you have an opportunity to enter in the correct direction. This does not mean you must take the signal—reflecting time after a trade (especially losing ventures) is important—but this is a valuable learning/reinforcement tool that will help train your eyes to assess the trend situation more accurately. If you do decide to take the trade, remember that it must always fit your predetermined risk/reward parameters.

Not every trade that you make will be a winner. But the goal of trading is not to be perfect. The goal of trading is to make money! By following these tenets and properly managing your trades from beginning to end, you will obtain the skills necessary to be consistently profitable because you will be functioning within a money-management system focused on *preserving capital*.

7

Bringing It All Together

Exploring Gann's Examples

Looking at my own copy of *How to Make Profits Trading in Commodities*, the first 63 1/2 pages are pure text, outlining the trading methodologies and rules. The rest of the book, through 412 pages, primarily illustrates examples of the tenets presented in the earlier chapters. Gann moves from wheat to soybeans through the rest of the commodities, giving specific examples of the rules in action.

In earlier works, such as *Truth of the Stock Tape* and *Wall Street Stock Selector*, Gann did include charts within chapters as he wrote and simultaneously analyzed them. However, in the *Commodities* book, the charts corresponding to each explanation are not located right up against the detailed wording. Through my years of study, this led me to think that Gann wanted me, the reader, to apply the words to the chart action myself, marking up my own chart to understand the rules at hand. In the end, when a trader goes to apply the rules, it is to the chart itself, so why didn't Gann mark the charts with the comments directly? I believe it's because he understands the power of practice in learning trading rules, and the simple fusion of the word description and the chart is the first step toward understanding what he set out to explain.

The 1940–1941 Soybean Trade

My father took this belief out a step by having me study one particular example of Gann's work over and over and over again: an example of a trade on soybean futures from the *Commodities* book. The original chart is located in Appendix D, "Gann's Soybean Chart."

One page 134, the relevant section begins as follows:

> TRADING EXAMPLES—Soy Beans—August 20, 1940, to October 16, 1941. See chart in back of book covering one- to three-day moves and volume of sales and open interest.

Note the mention of volume of sales and open interest. Gann doesn't refer to these in the trade example, as you'll see, but he obviously believed they were important. As you get a handle on the buying and selling points presented in this example, as well as the ones previously explored, adding volume and open interest to your charts will become invaluable.

Returning to Gann's writing, he goes on to say:

> These are examples of what could have been done by trading according to the rules. It is not my intention to lead anyone to believe that any average human being would get results of this kind, regardless of how well they understood the rules. The reason they would not buy and sell and make large profits of this kind is the HUMAN ELEMENT, which causes a man to act too often on hope and fear, instead of facing facts and following rules.

Gann is telling the reader that no "average" human being is destined to reap these results simply by following rules—something else will come into play. I understand "the HUMAN ELEMENT" to be any and all emotions that are grounded in hope and/or fear. Therefore, I believe that Gann is *not* saying that these results are unattainable; I believe he is saying that a human being who has mastered his reactions to emotions based on hope or fear is the type of person capable of achieving these results.

Moving forward to the actual trade analysis, Gann translates each glance at the chart into one line of text. I found that the best way to capitalize (educationally and, therefore, monetarily) on this setup was to do the following: After finding the chart that corresponds to the text, I used a large paper clasp to collect all the pages in between, to allow for easy flipping back and forth, from the trade descriptions to the actual chart. I have found this to be extremely helpful in matching more of Gann's verbal descriptions to the actual charts.

Back to finding the charts, when reading verbal descriptions of Gann's trade examples, it was natural to want to look at the actual chart while reading. However, instead of finding direction to the page number within the text, I had to return to a listing of charts that is an extension of the table of contents to find the correct chart. For this soybean example, when I finally found the chart for the first time, I wondered, "Why didn't Gann just refer to the page or chart number to begin with?" One answer is that he might have been unsure of how the charts would be numbered until he'd finished writing the book, and he could not go back to the text to mark references to aid the reader when searching for charts. Another possible answer is that he purposely left out the references so that the reader would have to scan the listing of charts to find the specific one he needed (in this case, "Chart No. 18—Soy Beans 1940 to 1941").

Returning to the text, the first set of trade actions reads:

> 1940—August 20—May Soy Beans, LOW 69C. The reason for buying was a triple bottom.
>
> We start with a capital of $1,000 which will margin 5,000 bushels of Soy Beans at 20c per bushel.
>
> Bought 5,000 May Soy Beans at 70c, placed stop loss order at 66.
>
> Risk limited to $200 and commission.

Gann says the signal was a triple bottom. However, flipping to Appendix D, you can see that there is no illustration of a triple bottom—only a line drawn just below the 70 horizontal marker. Therefore, it is impossible to know where the exact triple bottom points were, unless we could look at a chart with price data for every week or every day. Now, as someone who has reviewed this material many times, I contacted the Chicago Mercantile Exchange and attempted to retrieve a listing of the daily highs, lows, and closes for the May 1940 Soybean futures contract. On all occasions, I did not receive any follow-up, and after agonizing over my inability to obtain these exact records, I realized something: Gann wrote this book in 1942, most likely presuming that readers would have access to the rough data akin to the chart he drew out and that it would be sufficient. Who had time to call the exchange for more than a year's worth of daily soybean trading data just to better understand a textbook example?

This is why Gann presents many examples but shares charts in a basic manner, without many details. I believe that he was trying to show that the true lesson is in following the money management rules that are applied, as buy and sell signals appear in the examples. All the details I previously got hung up on, like having precise historical data, were not crucial to my learning of the lesson at hand.

So for every line of text relating Gann's commentary on a trade to the actual corresponding chart, I've come to use the following procedure to extract the most knowledge from the trade with the least amount of frustration. I explain the procedure using the next line of text in the soybean example as a model.

1. Read the line of text:

   October 8—Raised STOP LOSS ORDER to 74.

2. Ask yourself, "Why did Gann do this?" Asking this question early will help make decoding his examples a much easier task.

In this case, you would ask yourself, "Why was the stop loss raised?"

3. Immediately glance at the chart.

In this example, you see that that, on October 8, May soybean futures rallied through 79 cents and established a new higher base at 76 cents.

4. Mark any observations made, in the margin of the text, in a separate file of notes, or both.

For this example, I wrote "Raised stop to below latest bottom" in the margin.

Let's analyze the next line in the same fashion.

1. Read the line of text:

October 29—Raised STOP LOSS ORDER to 81 1/4. Keeping Stop Loss Orders 1c to 3c under bottoms.

2. Ask, "Why did Gann do this?"

In this example, the answer is pretty straightforward. A higher bottom formed, which is why the stop loss (protective stop order) was raised.

3. Immediately glance at the chart.

The chart shows that a higher low formed at 83 cents.

4. Mark any observations.

Here, I simply drew a line connecting my previous margin comment, "Raised stop to below latest bottom," to this example's line of text as well.

By moving through Gann's examples using these four steps, you will extract the most knowledge with the least amount of frustration. You will also zone in directly on the trade-management lessons that Gann was trying to convey through these many market examples.

Soybean Trade Re-created

Flipping back and forth between the text and chart is one way to associate Gann's description of a trade or market movements to its correlating chart. However, for in-depth study, I wanted to do something more thorough. I racked my brain for a way to make the chart material more useful to study. I wanted the chart itself to present more information that I could ascertain at a glance. I ultimately attempted to use a spreadsheet to re-create the charts using the given data along with the text descriptions.

By breaking down Gann's text into several key elements to tell the story of the trade, I plotted the trade action in the form of a Scatter chart (using Microsoft Excel) to create a new form of the commodity chart. The advantages of going through this process were that (a) it gave me a clear visual description of Gann's trade actions (whether historical or recommended) and (b) it forced me to immerse myself in the details of everything Gann laid out.

Examine Figure 7.1, representing the May 1941 soybeans sequence of trades described in the *Commodities* book (p. 134).

Note that I broke down the soybean trade information into eight components, as described in the chart legend. A look at the first set of markers on the far left of the chart explains how the rest of the markers came about:

In the middle of page 134 of the *Commodities* book, the text says:

> 1940—August 20—May Soy beans, LOW 69c. The reason for buying was a triple bottom.
>
> We start with a capital of $1,000, which will margin 5,000 bushels of Soy Beans at 20c per bushel.
>
> Bought 5,000 May Soy Beans at 70c, placed stop loss order at 66. Risk limited to $200 and commission.

Returning to the chart legend, the green solid diamond marker represents the price point (70 cents) and time point (August 20, 1940) at which the buy was entered (Buy Prices). (**Note:** Figures in the print book are grayscale, not color. To see the details of Figures 7.1 and 7.2 in color, go

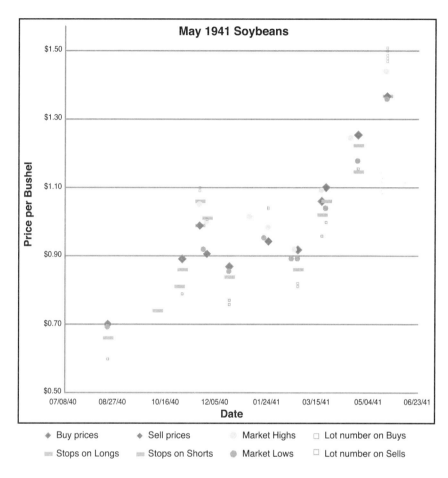

Figure 7.1 May 1941 Soybeans trade scatter chart

to the book's website at www.informit.com/title/9780132734387 and click the Sample Content tab.) The purple solid dot marker represents the low (69 cents) made on that same date (Market Lows). The solid pink dashed line marker represents the stop loss (protective stop) placed (at 66 cents) on that trade (Stops on Longs). Finally, the green square marker represents the number of lots that were traded. The minimum number of soybean futures contracts that can be traded is one, and one soybean future represents 5,000 bushels. Therefore, buying 5,000 bushels in this example (as explained by Gann) would equal one lot, so there is one green box marker (Lot number on Buys) on the Scatter chart. Buying 10,000 bushels would equal 2 lots, buying 15,000 bushels would equal 3 lots, and so on.

Continuing through the text in this manner yields the data necessary for the rest of the chart (see Tables 7.1 and 7.2).

Table 7.1 Data Inputs for May 1941 Soybean Trade

	High Made	**Low Made**
08/20/40		$ 0.69
11/18/40	$ 1.0500	
11/22/40		$ 0.9175
11/25/40	$ 1.0000	
12/18/40		$ 0.8550
01/07/41	$ 1.0150	
01/21/41		$ 0.9525
01/25/41	$ 0.9850	
02/18/41		$ 0.8925
02/21/41	$ 0.9200	
02/24/41		$ 0.8925
03/19/41	$ 1.0900	
03/23/41		$ 1.04
04/17/41	$ 1.2450	
04/24/41		$ 1.17625
05/21/41	$ 1.4388	
05/22/41		$ 1.36

The only columns that do not contain data directly from the text are the "Lot #" columns. I had to find a way to represent the number of lots bought and sold within the parameters of the x- and y-axes. Therefore, I decided to simply offset the lot number on buys and lot number on sells markers from the price per bushel at which the trade was made. For example, revisiting the first set of markers on the far left of the chart, the green square is positioned at the 60 cent level, an offset of 10 cents from the 70 cent buy entry price. If I had been selling at the 70 cent level, I would have placed a red square (lot number on sells marker) at the 80 cent level, again an offset of 10 cents, but this time placing the lot marker above the entry price marker (simply for visual ease).

Table 7.2 Data Inputs for May 1941 Soybean Trade

Date	Long			Short			
	Lot #	Price	Stop	Date	Lot #	Price	Stop
08/20/40	0.60	$0.7000	$0.6600				
10/08/40			$0.7400				
10/29/40			$0.8125				
11/01/40	0.79	$0.8900	$0.8600				
11/18/40			$0.9900				
				11/18/40	1.09	$0.9900	
				11/18/40	1.10	$0.9900	
				11/18/40	1.09	$0.9900	$1.0600
				11/25/40			$1.0100
				11/25/40	1.01	$0.9075	$1.0100
12/18/40	0.77	$0.8700					
12/18/40	0.76	$0.8700					
12/18/40	0.77	$0.8700	$0.8400				
				01/25/41	1.04	$0.9425	
				01/25/41	1.04	$0.9425	
02/24/41	0.82	$0.9200					
02/24/41	0.81	$0.9200					
02/24/41	0.82	$0.9200	$0.8600				

Table 7.2 Data Inputs for May 1941 Soybean Trade (continued)

	Long				Short		
Date	Lot #	Price	Stop	Date	Lot #	Price	Stop
02/24/41	0.81	$0.9200	$0.8600				
03/19/41	0.96	$1.0600	$1.0200				
03/23/41	1.00	$1.1000	$1.0600				
04/24/41			$1.1463				
04/24/41	1.16	$1.2550	$1.2250				
05/22/41			$1.3688	05/22/41	1.47	$1.3688	
				05/22/41	1.48	$1.3688	
				05/22/41	1.49	$1.3688	
				05/22/41	1.50	$1.3688	
				05/22/41	1.51	$1.3688	

With this information in place, I took this new chart out a step further. I added the lines of text relating to the buying and selling points and the trade-management rules in use directly to the chart using text boxes and arrows (see Figure 7.2).

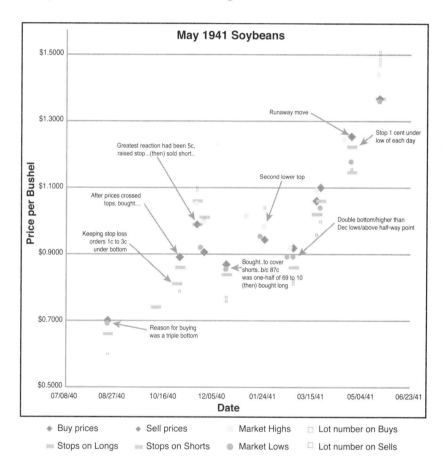

Figure 7.2 May 1941 Soybeans trade scatter chart with commentary

Overall, creating this chart and printing an annotated copy for regular review had educational value for me. Hopefully you can see how going through this exercise gave me a way to piece together many of the concepts explored earlier in this book into a tradable, usable fashion.

The best way for you to understand Gann's principles is to work through his examples. Your study doesn't have to be as elaborate as this soybean example, but it should not be as simple as reading through the example and setting it aside. Gann teaches through examples, so put your best learning methods to use to get inside his head.

When you've got a handle on how these signals and tenets play out in real-life examples, you can apply them to your own markets of study and observe the combinations and sequences of signals as they emerge.

Rigid Rules, Flexible Observation

Gann's buying and selling points and trading rules are presented with specific parameters to give you a framework to work within as a trader. However, one of the keys to successful trading is in being able to adapt to the market situation at hand.

With most trade setups, when you are "with the trend" (in a profitable trade), the trade moves in your direction almost immediately. If it doesn't, that is usually your first clue that you are in a losing trade. The beauty of Gann's trading methodologies is that they nicely fit within this framework. Certain clues can tell you relatively quickly whether the signal is going to play out as projected.

Take a look at Figure 7.3, of Corning. The market declined from $23.43 (February 4, 2011) to $11.51 (October 4, 2011) over the course of four sections down.

Zooming in toward $11.51, Figure 7.4 shows that the subsequent rise from the $11.51 bottom first tested the $15.59 resistance level (August 15, 2011 high) on October 27, 2011, reaching $15.62. However, the market posted a bearish test failure and returned to $13.71 (November 1, 2011 low). Another move higher took place, and strength retested the $15.59 key resistance one more, reaching $15.75 (November 15, 2011 high); however, a bearish test failure again formed. The market then reversed lower into a downtrend.

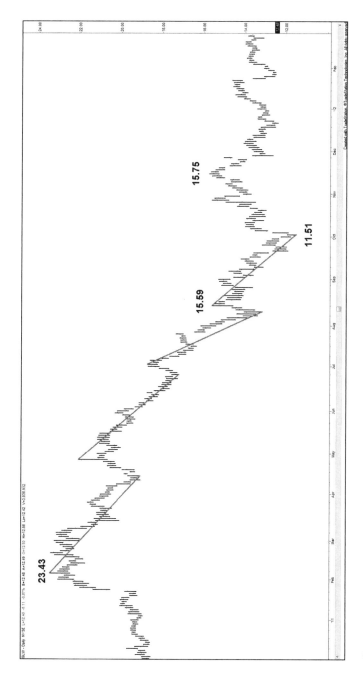

Charts created using TradeStation. ©TradeStation Technologies, Inc. 2001-2012. All rights reserved.

Figure 7.3 GLW, daily, as of April 25, 2012

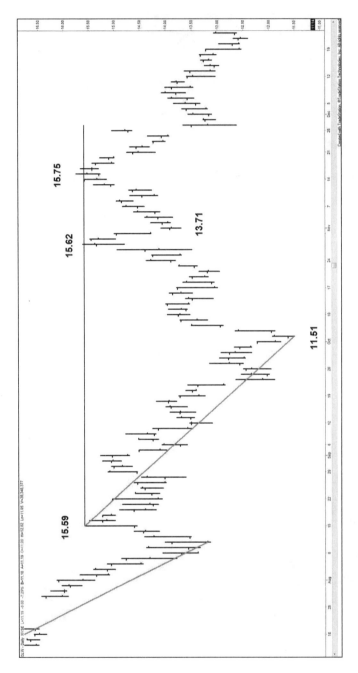

Charts created using TradeStation. ©TradeStation Technologies, Inc. 2001-2012. All rights reserved.

Figure 7.4 GLW, daily, as of December 23, 2011

The test failures were the first clues that this seemingly bullish setup was shaky. Other clues emerged as well. Look at the price action from the $11.51 low to the $15.75 high. Notice that it occurred in a series of sections, not one straight move, which would have indicated that greed had forcefully overcome fear and bulls were in control. This illustrates another way to confirm a signal, which is to look at the structure within the potential signal formation.

Another aspect of "rigid rules, flexible observation" shows up in how you perform your chart analysis. For example, when a tenet is presented and you are observing a 5-minute chart of a security, you must be flexible and willing to observe the security under different conditions. For example, when sections are not clear on that 5-minute chart, have the flexibility to move to a 1-minute chart or a 60-minute chart.

As you study the methods presented in this book within the context of your markets of interest, you will continue to discover the value of knowing the rules but being flexible as trading situations unfold.

8

Beyond Trading Basics

Looking to the Left of the Chart

Gann quoted King Solomon often, and one of the quotes he referred to was, "There is no new thing under the sun" (Ecclesiastes 1:9). If that's the case, then looking to the left of the chart, at the history of a market, has the potential to provide valuable insight into the future of that market.

That is what forecasting is all about. Now, I know I said that this book is about Gann's trading methodologies, not his forecasting work. However, I feel compelled to end this book with a brief foray into the importance of studying past price movement within a specified market. This is because Gann's most advanced (and prized) analysis methods all involve the study and observation of cycles within markets.

The key to understanding Gann's more complicated tools begins with understanding what a cycle actually is. According to *Merriam-Webster*'s online dictionary, the first definition of *cycle* is "an interval of time during which a sequence of a recurring succession of events or phenomena is completed." This definition mentions time, and this is the use of cycles most of us are familiar with, even outside of trading and the markets. We can examine the spans of our lifetimes and see how seasons change four times a year. We can examine our 24-hour day and see our sleeping and waking rhythms come into play. We can examine our government and see how actions repeat, with our major elections every four years. The list goes on and on.

To help you grasp Gann's advanced work, as you proceed with your study, you must understand that cycles apply to every aspect of our universe and to our trading, not just to time. In the case of the markets, cycles can be applied to price. This is why you see old bottoms become new tops (basis of Gann Selling Point #1) and old tops become new bottoms (Gann Buying Point #1). Definition 2a of *cycle* reinforces this point: "a course of series of events or operations that recur regularly and usually lead back to the starting point." It might seem at times that prices move haphazardly between zero and infinity, but they do "recur regularly" and "usually lead back to the starting point," depending on which point you are measuring from.

Definition 2b of *cycle* carries the word that is paramount to using cycles in forecasting: "one complete performance of a vibration, electric oscillation, current alternation, or other periodic process."

The magic word is *vibration*. Time vibrates. Price vibrates.

Measuring the vibrations of each market you follow is what forecasting is all about. I present some exercises to get you started in being aware of the vibration or rhythm within the market you trade.

The first step is to look at the OHLC chart of the security on a monthly or weekly basis. Start as early in the history of the price data as possible. The more data you can study into the past, the more you can determine about the future.

Using Google as an example, the stock was first traded on August 19, 2004. I've shared two weekly charts of Google. Figure 8.1 explores the first half of its 12-year life, and Figure 8.2 explores the second (or current) half.

The second step after acquiring trade data is to mark the significant highs and lows on the chart, especially the extreme high price and the extreme low price. Then use a separate daily chart to figure out the precise dates that match the high and low values.

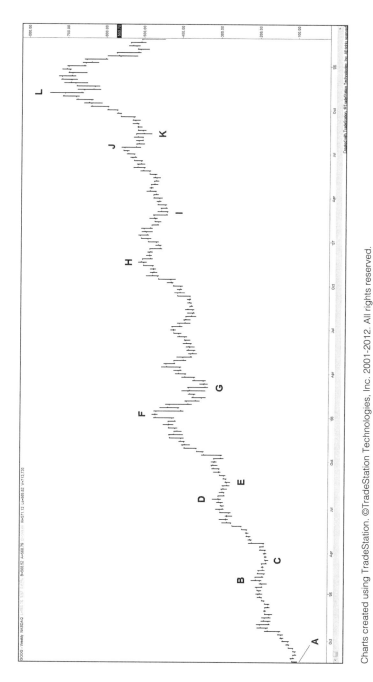

Charts created using TradeStation. ©TradeStation Technologies, Inc. 2001-2012. All rights reserved.

Figure 8.1 GOOG, weekly, as of February 22, 2008

A. $95.96 **extreme low** (August 19, 2004)

B. $216.80 high (February 2, 2005)

C. $172.57 low (March 14, 2005)

D. $317.80 high (July 21, 2005)

E. $273.35 low (August 22, 2005)

F. $475.11 high (January 11, 2006)

G. $331.55 low (March 10, 2006)

H. $513.00 high (November 22, 2006)

 I. $437.00 low (March 5, 2007)

 J. $558.58 high (July 16, 2007)

K. $480.46 low (August 16, 2007)

L. $747.24 **extreme high** (November 7, 2007)

M. $412.11 low (March 17, 2008)

N. $602.45 high (March 2, 2008)

O. $247.30 low (November 21, 2008)

P. $629.51 high (January 4, 2010)

Q. $433.63 low (July 1, 2010)

R. $642.92 high (January 19, 2011)

 S. $473.02 low (June 24, 2011)

T. $627.50 high (July 26, 2011)

U. $480.60 low (October 4, 2011)

V. $670.25 high (January 4, 2012)

Points A–V are listed in chronological order. However, if you flip to Appendix E, "Google, Inc., (GOOG) Highs and Lows by Calendar Month," you will find a list of the same high and low values, but organized by calendar month, from January to December.

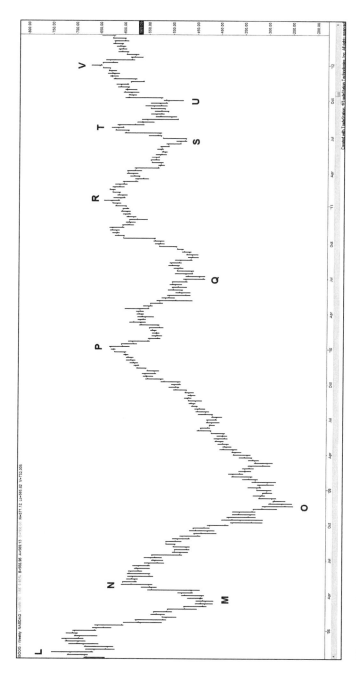

Figure 8.2 GOOG, weekly, as of March 16, 2012

Right off the bat, you should notice that some months contain several instances of significant highs or lows; other months are devoid of any major market turn during the entire history of trading of this stock.

The month of March shows five significant turns. January and July show four turns each. August and November show three turns each. So when trading this market into the future, would you expect significant changes in trend or market turns to occur during these months? Of course you would. You would not trade them blindly, but you would have awareness of the rhythm of this market, the beat to which it has been moving.

Similarly, note that no major trend changes took place in the months of April, May, September, and December. Would you expect turns to occur in those months ahead? Not likely.

Again, this is one of many ways to get to know the rhythm of your market. The more you make these types of observations and the more you study the relationships among highs and lows in the market, the more usable information you will uncover.

Recommended Reading

The first order of business for a serious student of Gann's works is to read through his original publications, as listed in Chapter 1, "The Work of W.D. Gann." As mentioned earlier in the book, it is helpful to study Gann's materials in the order in which he published them. Next, you can explore his specific market courses, depending on your area of interest: commodities, stocks, options, and so on. Additionally, you can read the books that Gann read himself, which are listed in a recommended reading list that Gann created. This list includes 81 titles, and the Lambert-Gann Publishing Company has reproduced 21 of them so far.

Gann spent a lifetime studying and reading about the markets. I am not saying that you need to do the same to use the valuable knowledge he shared. My intention is to provide you with a possible path of learning that you can adjust to your desire.

Obtaining Charts

Before you embark on (or return to) studying Gann's original works, I recommend taking time to collect five security charts. You can use your own charting software or free online sources. I've listed a few web sites that enable you to plot the types of charts I describe. Feel free to search out other web sites on your own; many exist.

www.freestockcharts.com

www.bigcharts.com

www.google.com/finance

You can save images of the charts in your charting software workspaces or use images from the online sources. However, I recommend having hard copies (printed) of the chart, whether you are accessing them digitally or have hard copies already in a trading newsletter or other chart-based publication. Make sure that you have one set of copies that you can mark up while keeping a clean set of originals.

As for the types of securities to choose for your charts, I believe you will get the most benefit in seeing the universal application of Gann's principles if you vary your charts. For example, you might choose to plot a stock, a commodity future, a currency, a fixed-income instrument, and a stock index future as your five securities. Vary the time frames you use. The choices are endless, but ideally, you want to see different degrees of market movement. For example, you might use a quarterly chart, a weekly chart, a daily chart, a 60-minute chart, and a 5-minute chart, instead of a 5-minute chart, a 4-minute chart, a 3-minute chart, a 2-minute chart, and a 1-minute chart.

As computer technology and graphic design continue to advance, the myriad chart styles available to traders and investors is vast and can be overwhelming. The most basic chart depicts the price action only—open, high, low, close (OHLC)—in the form of bars or candlesticks. Kagi charts incorporate volume into candlestick charts. Other trading systems color-code basic bar charts to extrapolate continuations or changes in trend based on each bar's directional movement. Many of these charts are useful to a variety of students of the market when combined with oscillators and other studies. However, these types of indicator-synthesizing charts are not crucial to understanding Gann's basic tenets. In fact, they might confuse a beginner student.

Therefore I recommend that you plot the charts as OHLC charts, as I've done with every example in this book. After you've plotted your charts as OHLC, create another set of charts of the same securities and time frames using Japanese Candlesticks, along with any other analysis tool with which you are familiar or would like to observe (moving average, MACD, and so on). Keep in mind that, for the purposes of practicing recognition of Gann's signals, it is best to plot any indicators separately on the chart (below the price bars), not overlay them on the price action.

Finally, I recommend keeping the colors of the charts simple, as I have done in this book. Use black OHLC bars against a white background. Some charting systems plot bars in green when the closing prices are above the opening prices, or plot in red for when the closing prices are below the opening prices. This might be helpful with your current trading, but it will likely confuse you in your initial practice of applying Gann's basic methods.

Gann's Writing Style and References

If you have already begun your study of Gann's materials, you probably understand why I am compelled to address his use of language. If you have not yet read any of Gann's materials, let me give you some examples of his style of writing, to clue you into what I believe was part of his strategy as an author.

The Holy Bible

The first quote from the Bible that Gann presents in his writings to the public is in his first book, *The Truth of the Stock Tape*. On page 51, he wrote, "The thing that hath been, it is that which shall be; and that which is done, is that which shall be done; and there is no new thing under the sun." (Ecclesiastes 1:9) Gann refers to the Bible many times throughout his works. Despite your religious (or not) convictions, it might be helpful to have a copy of the Bible to refer to as such quotes are mentioned. Pay close attention to all of Gann's Bible quotes—they are very near and dear to him, and he does not refer to them lightly.

Discussions of Mathematics

Gann often chooses famous quotes (often biblical ones) or creates his own phrases or sentences that discuss mathematics. To the casual reader, these might seem sprinkled into the book, but I believe that Gann purposefully placed these tenets as reminders of the greater realm within which trading and investing take place. It's all a game of supply and demand, which can be qualified and quantified. Anything that can be quantified is subject to the rules of the universe, which Gann clearly believes to be embedded in mathematics. Therefore, do not glaze over these statements or quotes when you approach them in Gann's text. Instead, begin to keep track of them on your own, and refer to them regularly to remind you that everything is happening in trading and investing within the context of the language of the universe: mathematics. Whether or not you believe this to be true, you will definitely benefit from the point of view to which this keeps you attuned.

Nothing Is Accidental

Gann once wrote the following: "When you make a trade, it must be on a good rule and for a good reason. There must be the possibility of a reasonable profit within a reasonable length of time .... The time limit to hold a Commodity depends upon the position you are in and the indication on your chart."[1]

When you read sentences such as these, don't be alarmed at the lack of detail. In my experience and study, Gann often writes such sentences mainly to bring your attention to an idea; he explains it later, usually through a real market example. The best way to deal with comments such as these is to not only highlight or underline them in the text, but to reiterate them in an independent outline of the key points from the chapters you are reading in any one book. By simply reprinting the line on another page, you acknowledge its importance. By reorganizing it into context with other similar tenets, you acknowledge its place. By reviewing it after all reading is said and done, you imprint it onto your brain—if that's not studying, I don't know what is!

Gann's use of uppercase font seems quite frequent. Take Gann's use of capitalization as an arrow pointing to information or ideas that he believes are important for you to understand and embrace. Be sure to incorporate these elements into your outline as you study.

Gann's arrangement of rules and descriptions throughout his text is unique, in that he does not always start with the most important items first. I believe that this is a step used to weed out the casual learner. How does it work? Well, for example, when Gann presented his list of buying points in the *Commodities* book, the casual learner might have read the first couple of signals listed, found them easy enough to understand, and then taken those rules to market

---

[1] W.D. Gann, *How to Make Profits Trading in Commodities* (Pomeroy, WA: Lambert-Gann, 2009), 14.

application, which often ends up being a premature move. However, the serious and dedicated learner would have read through an entire list of rules or ideas before attempting to apply any one of them. It has been my experience with Gann's works that, in this case, the student is rewarded duly. For example, the most crucial buy rule might come in the middle of a list of several, properly characterized by excessive use of capitalization and all. It can then be noted and highlighted as the most crucial rule and can be given top priority within the repertoire of signals learned from the readings. Basically, I believe through my study experience that Gann purposefully made the most important rules and ideas ones on which serious students would focus.

I believe that even the titling of some of Gann's books is done with great purpose. When I first came across *45 Years in Wall Street,* I assumed this to signify that Gann spent about 45 years studying the markets. But then I came across some facts about his life. The first was that, by the age of 24, he made his first trade in the commodities markets.[2] The second was that he wrote the book at the age of 72. Clearly, at the time, he had been involved with the markets for nearly 50 years, so why did he create a title highlighting 45 years? Well, referring back to the significance of eighths retracements on price, let's manipulate the eighths concept to time. We measure time in several ways, but the most straightforward is in calendar days. One year (Earth orbiting around the sun) is measured as approximately 365 days. During this time, the Earth moves in an elliptical orbit, 360° around the sun. What is one-eighth of 365 days? 45.625. And one-eighth of 360°? That's right, 45°. If you are familiar with Gann's works and are using this book to revisit basic ideas, you've probably already seen the significance of the measurement 45 in trading examples or trades of your own. If you are new to Gann's works, take this example as a strong hint to pay close attention to every aspect of each work.

---

[2] Billy Jones, *The W.D. Gann Technical Review* (Pomeroy, WA: Lambert-Gann, 2010), 1.

Again, Gann was a deliberate writer, and being aware of that as a student will greatly increase the value of your learning experience.

Lack of Fillers

Gann generally gets right to the point of what he is trying to convey. He states the teaching as he has learned it through his study and experience, and then he provides examples to illustrate it. At times, therefore, it might seem that reading his text is like reading an endless list of facts and tenets. This actually can make absorption of his material more difficult for some students; the brain has no time to rest and process if you read his text as if it is a narrative. Therefore, to help better absorb the material, especially at first when you are unfamiliar with this type of writing, pause (even just for a few seconds) after each page or even paragraph. Wrap your mind around what you just read before moving on to the next set of ideas.

Creating Affirmative Language

Gann writes more than a few sentences that speak right to the reader. He creates sentences starting with *You* that describe things you should or shouldn't be doing. To make those statements active and useful, turn them into affirmatives. This is what I did with the list of 28 rules, and you can apply it to any other aspect of Gann's works.

Again, keep a running list. For example, you can convert a sentence like "You should learn to trade on knowledge and eliminate fear and hope" (page 1 of the *Commodities* book) into "I trade on knowledge." Eventually, you will build a list of affirmative statements that reinforce Gann's tenets in your mind. The list will become helpful when you are in the "review" phases of trades, and even perhaps while you are managing them.

Even headings in the tables of contents in his books use "negative" language. In the *Commodities* book, just a few headings in, you read, "Human Element the Greatest Weakness," "What to Do When Commodities Are Going Against You," and "What to Do When You Have a Series of Losses." When you take notes on these chapters, using affirmative language helps you process the material. For example, under the heading "Time to Stay Out of the Market," be sure to focus on what Gann is trying to convey about times to *get into* the market.

Collect Your Own Examples

Just as Gann presents trading examples in great detail with the exact days, dates, and actions in his descriptions, do the same when you are ready to apply Gann's teachings to your charts. From the moment you come up with a trade idea, document it on its own. If the trade entry gets filled, note that as well. As the trade plays out, document the actions you take, as well as the reasons you take them, which should be part of your review process anyhow. In our modern world, we have the advantage of being able to apply notes directly to our computerized charts. Your annotations don't have to be long—just make them clear so that, upon reviewing the chart or text, you will know exactly what you did during that trade. In essence, I am asking you to track trades and examples as if you were going to write your own book delineating your trading methodologies. This will likely lead you to create a solid base of chart examples and text that add confidence to your future trading and that you can revisit and study to improve upon your skills.

A Study "Partner"—an Invaluable Tool

In my early days of learning about the markets and technical analysis, I had my father's guidance and mentorship. I also had him as a partner to review charts.

When I studied for my Chartered Market Technician (CMT) exam, I studied for Levels 1 and 2 mostly on my own, but I also worked with classmates from my exam preparation class. For Level 3, I reached out to other exam candidates and created a live study group. We studied together in person a few times, and we each brought in charts to share and compare ideas. Ultimately, every single person in my group passed the exam.

Why am I sharing this? I believe that study tools and groups should not be left behind after our academic days have passed. They can continue to provide a unique way to test our understanding of new material or refresh our brains on previously acquired knowledge.

I understand that many readers of this book—and, therefore, students of the markets—might find it daunting to find a study partner and pursue that learning relationship. But what's interesting is that you can become your own study partner by performing a few study tricks as you learn Gann's principles and apply them to charts.

First, remove identities. Using an image-editing program (every operating system generally comes with one, by default), edit out any labels on the chart that indicate the name of the security, the time axis, the price axis, or any other identifying information. You should ultimately be left with a series of unlabeled price bars. Set aside the chart for awhile and use it in a subsequent study session when you will no longer remember what label was there. By doing this exercise, your inherent view of a particular market based on fundamentals or current market conditions won't skew your analysis of the chart itself.

Second, turn the chart upside down. Rotate a printed chart clockwise until the original right side is now on the left and the original left side is now on the right. Figures 8.3 and 8.4 show examples of this; the first shows the original chart, and the second shows it in its manipulated state.

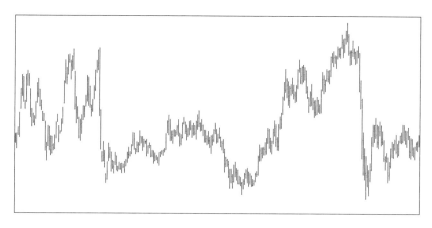

Figure 8.3 Example of blank chart for self-study

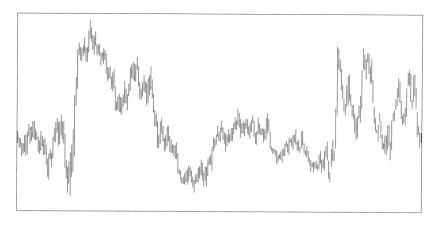

Figure 8.4 Example of blank chart for self-study after rotation

Again, because you're ignoring the labels, you have an easy way to neutralize a chart by turning a downtrend into an uptrend, and vice versa. Some people are inherent bulls or bears. But this exercise forces you to look at a market's price action in the reverse of what you just studied and analyzed. If you're an inherent bull and tend to bring up charts with uptrends to study, this gives you more downtrend examples. Understand that this is not a reflection of how the market trades—trends don't reverse into mirror images of the preceding price action. As I discussed earlier in the book, tops and bottoms do not form in exactly the same way. However, the general sections and patterns that form in the charts will still provide useful templates to become familiar with and be able to apply in future market analysis.

Third, revisit charts. Say that you intend to print several examples for immediate study. Be sure to print two copies of the same security and time frame. Mark up one of the copies with what you see as you first enter into Gann's teachings. Save the chart, along with its unmarked companion. Then when you are studying at a later phase in your learning, put those two charts back in front of you. If you simply see additional information to mark on the studied copy, go ahead and add the new information. However, if you see a set of patterns or signals that jump out at you in a new way, mark those observations on the blank copy. Date each chart every time you mark it up. As you continue to study Gann's materials, this will help you monitor every new concept that you learn.

The End...of the Beginning

We've explored several Gann tools in this book and can consider them in any market environment. Hopefully you can see that many of Gann's trading methodologies are straightforward enough to apply to your current market study. The Gann signals might work best for you when applied within the context of your existing trading toolbox—whether that includes oscillators, studies on the price chart, candlesticks, Fibonacci, or something else. Confluence is the key. Gann's methods are simple enough to add to other analysis tools already in play, as the subtitle of this book suggests.

Learning the buying and selling points is a bit like learning to ride a bicycle. You need to practice and get the hang of recognizing the signals. I recommended following them on paper before applying them to your live account. That's sort of like your training wheels. Then as you build confidence in your ability to recognize the patterns and plan sound trades around them (remember *capital preservation*), you can take off the training wheels and slowly incorporate these tools into your trading plan.

My goal in writing this book was to provide students like you a guide to mastering Gann's works. I wanted to write the book that didn't exist when I was 16 years old and was first handed the *Commodities* book by my father.

I hope that you have found value in what I've presented and that I've inspired you to take the next step toward trading success.

Gann's 28 Trading Rules

This is the original list from the book *How to Make Profits Trading in Commodities* with slight edits to account for additional wording used in the *45 Years on Wall Street* book.

#1. Amount of capital to use: Divide your capital into ten equal parts, and never risk more than one-tenth of your capital on any one trade.

#2. Use stop loss orders. Always protect a trade when you make it with a stop loss order 1 to 3 cents, never more than 5 cents away. Cotton 20 to 40, never more than 60 points away; 3 to 5 points away for stocks.

#3. Never overtrade. This would be violating your capital rules.

#4. Never let a profit run into a loss. After you once have a profit of 3 cents or more, raise your stop loss order so that you will have no loss of capital. For cotton, when the profits are 60 points or more, place a stop where there will be no loss.

#5. Do not buck the trend. Never buy or sell if you are not sure of the trend according to your charts and rules.

#6. When in doubt, get out, and don't get in when in doubt.

#7. Trade only in active markets. Keep out of slow, dead ones.

#8. Equal distribution of risk. Trade in two or three different commodities, if possible. (Trade in four or five stocks, if possible.) Avoid tying up all your capital in any one commodity.

#9. Never limit your orders or fix a buying or selling price. Trade at the market.

#10. Don't close your trades without a good reason. Follow up with a stop loss order to protect your profits.

#11. Accumulate a surplus. After you have made a series of successful trades, put some money into a surplus account to be used only in emergency or in times of panic.

#12. Never buy or sell just to get a scalping profit.

#13. Never average a loss. This is one of the worst mistakes a trader can make.

#14. Never get out of the market just because you have lost patience or get into the market because you are anxious from waiting.

#15. Avoid taking small profits and big losses.

#16. Never cancel a stop loss order after you have placed it at the time you make a trade.

#17. Avoid getting in and out of the market too often.

#18. Be just as willing to sell short as you are to buy. Let your object be to keep with the trend and make money.

#19. Never buy just because the price of a commodity is low or sell short just because the price is high.

#20. Be careful about pyramiding at the wrong time. Wait until the commodity is very active and has crossed Resistance Levels before buying more and until it has broken out of the zone of distribution before selling more.

#21. Select the commodities that show strong uptrend to pyramid on the buying side and the ones that show definite downtrend to sell short.

#22. Never hedge. If you are long of one commodity and it starts to go down, do not sell another commodity short to hedge it. Get out at the market; take your loss and wait for another opportunity.

#23. Never change your position in the market without good reason. When you make a trade, let it be for some good reason or according to some definite rule; then do not get out without a definite indication of a change in trend.

#24. Avoid increasing your trading after a long period of success or a period of profitable trades.

#25. Don't guess when the market is top. Let the market prove it is top. Don't guess when the market is bottom. Let the market prove it is bottom. By following definite rules, you can do this.

#26. Do not follow another man's advice unless you know that he knows more than you do.

#27. Reduce trading after the first loss; never increase.

#28. Avoid getting in wrong and out wrong, getting in right and out wrong; this is making double mistakes.

B

Affirmative Versions of Gann's 28 Rules

Gann Rule (Affirmative) #1: Divide your capital into ten equal parts and always risk less than one-tenth of your capital on any one trade.

Gann Rule (Affirmative) #2: Use stop loss orders. Always protect a trade when you make it (on commodities) with a stop loss order 1 to 3 cents (up to 5 cents) away—for cotton, 20 to 40 points (up to 60 points) away; for stocks, 3 to 5 points away.

Gann Rule (Affirmative) #3: Always trade lot sizes and amounts of risk that fit within the limits of your capital.

Gann Rule (Affirmative) #4: Always protect your accumulated profit. On a long position, raise your stop loss order once your profit equals your initial risk. On a short position, lower your stop loss order once your profit equals your initial risk.

Gann Rule (Affirmative) #5: Trade with the trend. Buy or sell only if you are sure of the trend, according to your chart and rules.

Gann Rule (Affirmative) #6: Enter the market and stay in a trade only as long as you are sure of the market indications according to your rules.

Gann Rule (Affirmative) #7: Trade only in active markets.

Gann Rule (Affirmative) #8: Distribute risk equally among traded markets. Risk only up to 10% of your capital in any one market.

Gann Rule (Affirmative) #9: Let the market show you at what price to enter a buy or a sell.

Gann Rule (Affirmative) #10: Close your trade only with a good reason. Follow up with a stop loss order to protect your profits.

Gann Rule (Affirmative) #11: Accumulate a surplus. After you have made a series of successful trades, put some money into a surplus account as an emergency fund.

Gann Rule (Affirmative) #12: Trade the swings in accordance with the existing trend. This is where you can make the most profit for the fewest trades.

Gann Rule (Affirmative) #13: Pyramid only on trades that are showing profit. This is how you can make the most profits on sustained moves.

Gann Rule (Affirmative) #14: Enter and exit the market only on definite signals, with emotions in check.

Gann Rule (Affirmative) #15: Take large profits and small losses.

Gann Rule (Affirmative) #16: After you've placed a stop loss order, always keep it, and move it only in the direction that minimizes risk/protects profits.

Gann Rule (Affirmative) #17: Trade only when you have definite signals.

Gann Rule (Affirmative) #18: Be just as willing to sell short as you are to buy. Let your object be to keep with the trend and make money.

Gann Rule (Affirmative) #19: Buy only when you have definite indication of a rising market. Sell only when you have definite indication of a falling market.

Gann Rule (Affirmative) #20: Pyramid at the right time. On a long position, wait until the security is very active and has crossed Resistance Levels before buying more. On a short position, wait until the security has broken out of the zone of distribution before selling more.

Gann Rule (Affirmative) #21: Select the commodities that show strong uptrend to pyramid on the buying side and the ones that show definite downtrend to sell short.

Gann Rule (Affirmative) #22: If you have a position on and the market starts to move against it, get out at the market, take your loss, and wait for another opportunity. Or rely on your stop order to minimize your losses.

Gann Rule (Affirmative) #23: Change your position in the market only with a good reason. When you make a trade, let it be for some good reason or according to some definite rule; then stay in the trade until you have a definite indication of a change in trend.

Gann Rule (Affirmative) #24: Maintain your lot size and maximum risk amount after a long period of success or a period of profitable trades. (Increase your lot size and maximum risk amount only after you have doubled your capital and added back half to your initial account size, increasing your total tradable capital amount.)

Gann Rule (Affirmative) #25: Let the market prove it is making a top. Let the market prove it is making a bottom. By following definite rules, you can do this.

Gann Rule (Affirmative) #26: Only follow another man's advice if you know that he knows more than you do.

Gann Rule (Affirmative) #27: If your lot size contains multiple contracts, reduce the number of contracts traded after the first loss.

Gann Rule (Affirmative) #28: Focus on getting in the market according to your rules and out of the market according to your rules.

C

Gann's Buying and Selling Points

Gann Buying Point #1: BUY at OLD BOTTOMS or OLD TOPS. When a commodity declines to an OLD BOTTOM or to an OLD TOP, it is always a buying point with a STOP LOSS ORDER. In fact, you should never buy unless you can figure where to place a STOP LOSS ORDER 1 cent to 3 cents away and when commodities are selling at high prices, never more than 5 cents away ....

Gann Buying Point #2: SAFER BUYING POINT. Buy when wheat, cotton, or any commodity crosses a series of tops of previous weeks, showing that the minor or the main trend has turned up as indicated by the charts on individual commodities.

Gann Buying Point #3: SAFEST BUYING POINT. Buy on a secondary reaction after wheat, cotton, or any commodity has crossed previous weekly tops and the advance exceeds the greatest rally on the way down from the top.

Gann Buying Point #4: BUY when the first rally from the extreme bottom exceeds in time the greatest rally in the preceding Bear Campaign.

Gann Buying Point #5: BUY when the period of time exceeds the last rally before extreme lows were reached. If the last rally was 3 or 4 weeks, when the advance from the bottom is more than 3 or 4 weeks, consider the trend has turned up and commodities are a safer buy on a secondary reaction.

Gann Buying Point #6: BUY AFTER BREAKAWAY POINTS ARE CROSSED ON INDIVIDUAL COMMODITIES. The market will then be in the runaway move where you can make large profits in a short period of time.

Gann Buying Point #7: BUY when wheat, corn, cotton, or any commodity declines to 50% of highest selling prices, or to 1/2 or 50% range between extreme high or extreme low prices. This is one of the safe buying points, as we will prove later by examples of past market movements. When there is a 50% reaction of the last move up, it becomes a buying point so long as the main trend is up ....

Gann Buying Point #8: BUY against double or triple bottoms, or buy on first, second, or third higher bottom and buy a second lot after wheat, soybeans, or cotton makes second or third higher bottom, then crosses previous top.

Gann Buying Point #9: BUYING RULES FOR RAPID ADVANCES AT HIGH LEVELS. In the last stages of a Bull Market in a commodity, reactions are small. Buy on 2-day reactions and follow up with STOP LOSS ORDER 1 cent to 2 cents under each day's low level. Then when the low of a previous day is broken, you will be out. Markets sometimes run 10 to 30 days without breaking low of previous day.

Gann Selling Point #1: SELL at OLD TOPS or OLD BOTTOMS. An important point to sell out longs and sell short is at OLD TOPS or when wheat or commodities rally to OLD BOTTOMS the first, second, or third time...

Gann Selling Point #2: SAFER SELLING POINT. Sell when wheat, soybeans, cotton, or any commodity breaks the low of a previous week or a series of bottoms of previous weeks as indicated by the trend and rules.

Gann Selling Point #3: SAFEST SELLING POINT. Sell on a *secondary rally* after wheat, soybeans, cotton, or any commodity has broken the previous bottoms of several weeks or has broken the bottom of the last reaction, turning trend down. This *secondary rally* nearly always comes after the first sharp decline in the first section of Bear Campaign.

Gann Selling Point #4: SELL after the first decline exceeds the greatest reaction in the preceding Bull Campaign or the last reaction before final top.

Gann Selling Point #5: Sell after BREAKAWAY POINT is crossed.

Gann Selling Point #6: Sell when the period of time of the first decline exceeds the last reaction before final top of the Bull Campaign. Example: If wheat or any commodity has advanced for several months of for one year of more, and the greatest reaction has been 4 weeks, which is an average reaction in a Bull Market, then after top is reached and the first decline runs more than 4 weeks, it is an indication of a change in the minor trend or the main trend. The commodity will be a safer short sale on any rally because you will be trading with the trend after it has been definitely defined.

Gann Selling Point #7: SELL at 50% or 1/2 point of last high to low of sharp decline or sell at 50% of highest selling point or 50% of greatest range. Sell when wheat, soybeans, cotton, or any commodity rallies 50% of a previous move down ....

Gann Selling Point #8: SELL against Double Tops or Triple Tops, or SELL when the market makes lower tops or lower bottoms. It is safe to sell when wheat, soybeans, or cotton makes a second, third, or fourth lower top; also safe to sell after *double* and *triple bottoms* are broken.

Gann Selling Point #9: SELL in the last stages of Bear Market or when there is rapid decline and only 2 days' rallies, and follow down with stop loss order 1 cent above the high of the previous day. When wheat or any commodity rallies 1 cent or more above the high of the previous day, you will be out on *stop*. Fast-declining markets will often run 10 to 30 days without crossing the high of the previous day.

D

Gann's Soybean Chart

How to Make Profits in Commodities, page 351, by W.D. Gann. Courtesy of Nikki Jones, Lambert-Gann Publishing Co. 2012.

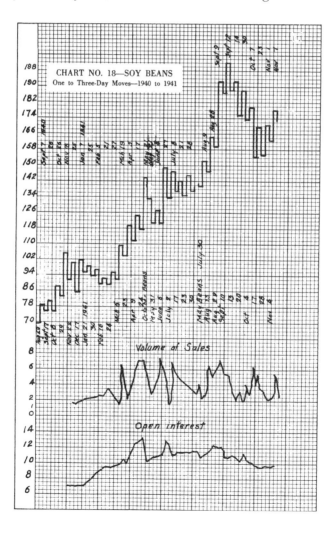

E

Google, Inc. (GOOG) Highs and Lows by Calendar Month

January
F: $475.11 high (January 11, 2006)
P: $629.51 high (January 4, 2010)
R: $642.92 high (January 19, 2011)
V: $670.25 high (January 4, 2012)

February
B: $216.80 high (February 2, 2005)

March
C: $172.57 low (March 14, 2005)
G: $331.55 low (March 10, 2006)
I: $437.00 low (March 5, 2007)
M: $412.11 low (March 17, 2008)
N: $602.45 high (March 2, 2008)

April

May

June
S: $473.02 low (June 24, 2011)

July
D: $317.80 high (July 21, 2005)
J: $558.58 high (July 16, 2007)
Q: $433.63 low (July 1, 2010)
T: $627.50 high (July 26, 2011)

August

A: $95.96 extreme low (August 19, 2004)

E: $273.35 low (August 22, 2005)

K: $480.46 low (August 16, 2007)

September

October

U: $480.60 low (October 4, 2011)

November

L: $747.24 extreme high (November 7, 2007)

H: $513.00 high (November 22, 2006)

O: $247.30 low (November 21, 2008)

December

Index

NUMBERS

100% retracements, 86
1940-1941 soybean trades, 140-150
45 Years in Wall Street, 4, 165
50% retracements, 86

A

accounts
  stop loss orders, 124
  trading, 121. *See also* trading
accumulation, 79-81
actions
  bars, 108
  cycles, 88
  prices, 12, 109. *See also* prices
    time constructs, 22
    triple bottoms, 51
    volatility, 114
    weekly, 63
  radius of, 29
  trading, 78
advances, 9
advice, 7
  money-management, 121
affirmative rules, 40. *See also rules*
  Gann Rule (Affirmative) #1, 120, 177

Gann Rule (Affirmative) #2, 123, 177
Gann Rule (Affirmative) #3, 121, 177
Gann Rule (Affirmative) #4, 128, 177
Gann Rule (Affirmative) #5, 40, 177
Gann Rule (Affirmative) #6, 127, 177
Gann Rule (Affirmative) #7, 40, 177
Gann Rule (Affirmative) #8, 122, 177
Gann Rule (Affirmative) #9, 126, 177
Gann Rule (Affirmative) #10, 135, 178
Gann Rule (Affirmative) #11, 121, 178
Gann Rule (Affirmative) #12, 41, 178
Gann Rule (Affirmative) #13, 127, 178
Gann Rule (Affirmative) #14, 123, 178
Gann Rule (Affirmative) #15, 137, 178
Gann Rule (Affirmative) #16, 123, 178

Gann Rule (Affirmative) #17, 41, 178

Gann Rule (Affirmative) #18, 41, 178

Gann Rule (Affirmative) #19, 41, 178

Gann Rule (Affirmative) #20, 127, 178

Gann Rule (Affirmative) #21, 127, 178

Gann Rule (Affirmative) #22, 136, 179

Gann Rule (Affirmative) #23, 127, 179

Gann Rule (Affirmative) #24, 137, 179

Gann Rule (Affirmative) #25, 49, 179

Gann Rule (Affirmative) #26, 179

Gann Rule (Affirmative) #27, 137, 179

Gann Rule (Affirmative) #28, 135, 179

agreements, 114. *See also* closing prices

Alcatel Lucent, 88, 92

American Mobil, 57

analysis
  markets, 2, 12
  oscillators, 104-108
  patterns, 13-20
  principles outside of price, 95-108
  time, 87
  trendlines, 95-103
  triple bottoms/tops, 49

applications
  Gann's principles. *See* principles (Gann's)
  TradeStation, 11

applying Gann's principles, 85
  favorite numbers, 85-92
  importance of closing prices, 108-117
  outside of price, 95-108

articles, 1

assessment
  risk, 120-122
  stop loss orders, 124
  trends, 39

AUDUSD (Australian dollar/U.S. dollar), 36

B

Bank of America, 108

bars
  actions, OHLC (open high low close), 108
  plotting, 11
  prices, 90
  stop loss orders, 131
  two-bar rules, 130

basic movement of markets, 9-11

bear markets, 9, 39. *See also* markets
  duration, 42
  prices, exceeding moves in, 63
  rapid moves, 76

Bible quotes, 163

books. *See* publications

bottoms
  double, 57-62
  sell old, 69-74
  triple, 49-54

boundaries, consolidation, 83

breakevens, managing, 128

breakouts, 81, 83

bull markets, 9, 39. *See also*
  markets
    corrections, 48
    Gann selling point #6, 48
buying, 12, 40
    buy old tops/sell old bottoms,
      69-74
    points, 79, 181-183
      exiting, 136
      Gann Rule #1, 69, 156, 181
      Gann Rule #2, 181
      Gann Rule #3, 63, 181
      Gann Rule #4, 41, 42, 181
      Gann Rule #5, 44, 104, 181
      Gann Rule #6, 182
      Gann Rule #7, 182
      Gann Rule #8, 49, 57,
        124, 182
      Gann Rule #9, 74, 182

C

calculations
    strengths, 33
    time, 87
calculators, inflation, 4
capital, managing, 119
    placement of orders, 123-126
    reviewing, 136-138
    risk assessment, 120-122
    trade initiations, 126
ceilings
    prices, 31
    removing, 79
center axis, 100
charts
    Alcatel Lucent, 88, 92
    Clearwire Corporation, 72
    Corn futures, 90
    Corning, 150
    Elements of the Market, 44
    E-mini S&P 500 futures, 97

    examples, 168
    formatting, 162
    Gap, Inc., 70
    Gold Cash Index, 114
    Google, 97, 100, 156-160
    Juniper Networks, 65
    Micron Technology, 54
    NZDUSD, 14
    obtaining, 161-162
    OHLC (open high low close),
      111, 156
    Pfizer, Inc., 88
    Pitney Bowes, 105
    plotting, 162
    price exercise, 27
    security, 11
    soybean futures, 76, 130
    stocks, 28
    sugar futures, 104
    tools, 97
    trade examples (1940-1941
      soybean futures), 140-150
    trading, 155-160
    trendlines, 95-103
Cisco Systems, 49
clear trends, 33. *See also* **trends**
Clearwire Corporation, 72
closing prices, importance of,
    108-117
clusters, retracements, 86
colors, charts, 162
commodities
    comparisons to gambling, 5
    futures (wheat), 2
Commodity course, 4
confirmation of trendlines, 100
consolidation
    50% retracement levels, 88
    boundaries, 83
    movements, 82
    zones, 100

constructs, time, 20-26
corn futures, 90
Corning, 150
corrections
  downtrends, 81
  duration, 48
  reactions, 74
  size of, 44
  time, 42
courses, 4
cycles, 155-156
  market actions, 88

D

declines, 9
  Cisco Systems, 49
  corrections, 44. *See also*
    corrections
  fast-declining markets, 76
directional movement, 95. *See
  also* trendlines
discounts, prices, 12
distribution, 81
diversification, 122
double bottoms/tops, 57-62
down trendlines, 96
downtrends, 33, 74, 79. *See also*
  trends
duration, 41. *See also* time
  bear markets, 42
  corrections, 48
  triple bottoms, 51-53

E

eighths retracement levels, 30,
  33, 90-92
  100%, 86
  50%, 86
  importance of closing prices, 117

elements of markets, 9
  basic movement of, 9-11
  prices, 11-12
  repeating patterns, 12-20
  time, 20-26
Elements of the Market chart, 44
emergency funds, 121
E-mini S&P 500 futures, 97, 125
entry into markets, 79
  oscillators, 104
equality, 29
erratic price movements, 12
examples, 139, 167
  charts, 168
exceeding moves
  in price, 63-68
  in time, 41
exercises, stock charts, 28
existing price movements,
  projections based on, 32-38
exiting from markets, 79, 135-136
  oscillators, 104
  signals, understanding, 111

F

Face Facts America, 4
failures, testing, 111
fast-declining markets, 76
favorite numbers, applying
  Gann's principles, 85-92
fear, 53
fluctuation of price, 27-31
following advice, 7
forecasting, 1, 5, 155. *See also*
  predictions
formatting
  charts, 162
  OHLC (open high low
    close), 162
four-section bear markets, 10

four-section bull markets, 10
futures
    commodities (wheat), 2
    corn, 90
    E-mini S&P 500, 97, 125
    soybeans, 130, 185
        1940-1941 trades
          (examples), 140-150
        charts, 76
    sugar, 104

G

gambling, comparisons to, 5
Gann, W.D., 1-5
Gap, Inc., 70
Gilley, William E., 1-4
Gold Cash Index, 114
Google, 42, 187-188
    charts, 97, 100, 156-160
greed, 53
guidelines. *See also* managing
    account management, 121
    capital-management, 125

H

high prices. *See also* prices;
  ranges
    100% retracements, 86
    50% retracements, 86-93
    charts, 111
    managing, 129
Honeywell International, 63
horizontal lines, 30
How to Make Profits Trading in
  Commodities, xvii, 4, 6, 40
How to Make Profits Trading in
  Puts and Calls, 4
human element, 141

I

importance of closing prices,
  108-117
indexes
    Gold Cash Index, 114
    RSI (Relative Strength Index),
      104, 105
    S&P 500 Cash Index, 46
indicators, oscillators, 104-108
inflation calculators, 4
initiation of trades, 126
interpreting markets, 27
    projections based on existing
      price movements, 32-38
    view of price movement, 27-31
intraday levels, 22

J

Jones, Nikki, xv-xvi
Juniper Networks, 65

L

Lambert-Gann Publishing
  Company, 4, 160
levels
    eighths retracement, 30, 33, 86,
      90-92
    intraday, 22
    triple tops, 54
limitations of trendlines, 97
lines
    horizontal, 30
    segments, 29
locations, significant, 28
long positions, 79
    stop loss orders, 124
losses. *See also* stop loss orders
    minimizing, 111, 137
    risk assessment, 121

low prices. *See also* prices; ranges
100% retracements, 86
50% retracements, 86-93
charts, 111
managing, 129

M

Magic Word, 4
managing
breakevens, 128
capital, 119
trading, 79, 119, 127-135
exiting, 135-136
placement of orders,
123-126
reviewing, 136-138
risk assessment, 120-122
trade initiations, 126
markets
actions, cycles, 88
analysis, 2, 12
bear. *See* bear markets
bull. *See* bull markets
elements of, 9
basic movement of, 9-11
prices, 11-12
repeating patterns, 12-20
time, 20-26
exiting from, 135-136
importance of closing prices, 117
interpreting, 27
projections based on existing
price movements, 32-38
view of price movement,
27-31
predictions, 1-3
retracements
100%, 86
50%, 86-93

trading, 39
buy old tops/sell old
bottoms, 69-74
double bottoms/tops, 57-62
exceeding moves in
price, 63-68
exceeding moves in
time, 41
ranges, 79-83
rapid moves, 74-80
triple bottoms/tops, 49-54
mathematics, 163
maximizing profits, 111
measurements
50% retracements, 90
prices, 11, 21
retracements, 38
time, 87. *See also* time
vibrations, 156
mentorships, 167-170
methodologies, 5, 40
Micron Technology
double bottoms/tops, 61
triple bottoms/tops, 54
midpoints, 29
minimizing losses, 111, 137
movement
oscillators, 104
prices, 13, 27-31
trendlines, 95-103
movements
consolidation, 82
of markets, 9-11
prices, projections based on
existing, 32-38
sideways price, 79
Murphy, John J., 95

N

National Squares Calculator course workbook, 2
never-failing trading rules, 6. *See also* rules
news stories, effects on prices, 12
New Stock Trend Detector, 4
numbers, Gann's favorite, 85-92

O

obtaining charts, 161-162
OHLC (open high low close), 11, 108, 156, 162
  charts, 111
orders, placement of, 123-126
oscillators, 104-108

P

parameters of rules, 150-152
patterns
  double bottoms/tops, 57-62
  oscillators, 104
  repeating, 12-20
  triple bottoms/tops, 49-54
percentages, 30
  of capital to risk, 120
  levels, 30
Pfizer, Inc., 88
Pitney Bowes, 42, 106
pivots, prices, 106, 108
placement of orders, 123-126
  retracements, 129
plotting
  charts, 162
  price bars, 11
  stocks, 161

points
  buying, 181-183. *See also* buying points
  pressure, 90
  selling, 181-183. *See also* selling points
positions, long, 79
predictions, markets, 1-3
pressure points, 90
prices, 11-12
  actions, 109
    triple bottoms, 51
    volatility, 114
    weekly, 63
  bars, 11, 90
  ceilings, 31
  closing, importance of, 108-117
  discounts, 12
  exceeding moves in, 63-68
  measurements, 11, 21
  movement, 13
    past, studying, 155
    projections based on existing, 32-38
    view if, 27-31
  oscillators, 104-108
  pivots, 106, 108
  principles outside of, 95-108
  sideways price movements, 79
  targets, 33
principles (Gann's), 85
  favorite numbers, 85-92
  importance of closing prices, 108-117
  outside of price, 95-108
profits, 137
  maximizing, 111
  risk assessment, 121
  stop loss orders, 135
  trends, 40

projections, based on existing
price movements, 32-38
publications, 3-5
   45 Years in Wall Street, 4, 165
   Face Facts America, 4
   *How to Make Profits Trading in
   Commodities*, 4
   *How to Make Profits Trading in
   Puts and Calls*, 4
   Magic Word, 4
   *National Squares Calculator
   course workbook*, 2
   New Stock Trend Detector, 4
   Ticker and Investment Digest, 1
   Truth of the Stock Tape, 4, 163
   Tunnel Thru the Air, 4
   Wall Street Stock Selector, 4

R

radius of action, 29
rallies, 31
   old bottoms, 72
   oscillators, 105
   S&P 500 Cash Index, 46
   time, 41
   trendlines, 100
random consolidation, 82
ranges
   100% retracements, 86
   50% retracements, 86-93
   prices, 63. *See also* prices
   trading, 79-83
rapid moves, 74-80
reactions, rapid moves, 74
reading
   charts, 155-160
   recommended, 160-161
rebounds, triple tops, 54
recommended reading, 160-161
references, 162-167

relationships, 13
Relative Strength Index. *See* RSI
repeating patterns, 12-20
resistance, 31, 38, 108
retracements. *See also* eighths
   retracement levels
   100%, 86
   50%, 86-93
   breakevens, managing, 128
   eighths levels, 86, 90-92
   importance of closing prices, 117
   measurements, 38
   projection, 33
reversals, 50% retracement
   levels, 92
reviewing trade management,
   136-138
rigid rules, 150-152
risk assessment, 120-122
RSI (Relative Strength Index),
   104, 105
rules
   exiting, 136
   Gann Rule (Affirmative) #1,
   120, 177
   Gann Rule (Affirmative) #2,
   123, 177
   Gann Rule (Affirmative) #3,
   121, 177
   Gann Rule (Affirmative) #4,
   128, 177
   Gann Rule (Affirmative) #5,
   40, 177
   Gann Rule (Affirmative) #6,
   127, 177
   Gann Rule (Affirmative) #7,
   40, 177
   Gann Rule (Affirmative) #8,
   122, 177
   Gann Rule (Affirmative) #9,
   126, 177

Gann Rule (Affirmative) #10, 135, 178

Gann Rule (Affirmative) #11, 121, 178

Gann Rule (Affirmative) #12, 41, 178

Gann Rule (Affirmative) #13, 127, 178

Gann Rule (Affirmative) #14, 123, 178

Gann Rule (Affirmative) #15, 137, 178

Gann Rule (Affirmative) #16, 123, 178

Gann Rule (Affirmative) #17, 41, 178

Gann Rule (Affirmative) #18, 41, 178

Gann Rule (Affirmative) #19, 41, 178

Gann Rule (Affirmative) #20, 127, 178

Gann Rule (Affirmative) #21, 127, 178

Gann Rule (Affirmative) #22, 136, 179

Gann Rule (Affirmative) #23, 127, 179

Gann Rule (Affirmative) #24, 137, 179

Gann Rule (Affirmative) #25, 49, 179

Gann Rule (Affirmative) #26, 7, 179

Gann Rule (Affirmative) #27, 137

Gann Rule (Affirmative) #28, 135, 179

Gann trading rule #1, 173

Gann trading rule #2, 173

Gann trading rule #3, 173

Gann trading rule #4, 173

Gann trading rule #5, 173

Gann trading rule #6, 173

Gann trading rule #7, 173

Gann trading rule #8, 173

Gann trading rule #9, 173

Gann trading rule #10, 174

Gann trading rule #11, 174

Gann trading rule #12, 174

Gann trading rule #13, 174

Gann trading rule #14, 174

Gann trading rule #15, 174

Gann trading rule #16, 174

Gann trading rule #17, 174

Gann trading rule #18, 174

Gann trading rule #19, 174

Gann trading rule #20, 174

Gann trading rule #21, 174

Gann trading rule #22, 174

Gann trading rule #23, 175

Gann trading rule #24, 175

Gann trading rule #25, 175

Gann trading rule #26, 175

Gann trading rule #27, 175

Gann trading rule #28, 175

parameters of, 150-152

price action, 22

stop loss orders, 131

trading, 6-7

two-bar, 130

runaway moves, 129-135

S

savings funds, 121

scatter charts, 149. *See also* charts

securities, types of, 161

security charts, 11, 161

segments, lines, 29

self-study, 168

selling, 12, 40
  buy old tops/sell old bottoms,
    69-74
  points, 79, 181-183
    exiting, 136
    Gann Rule #1, 70, 72,
      156, 182
    Gann Rule #2, 182
    Gann Rule #3, 65-66,
      105, 182
    Gann Rule #4, 42, 183
    Gann Rule #5, 183
    Gann Rule #6, 48, 183
    Gann Rule #7, 183
    Gann Rule #8, 53, 61, 183
    Gann Rule #9, 76, 78, 183
sessions, trading, 114. *See also*
  trading
short-term trade opportunities, 83
  boundaries, 83
  oscillators, 104
  retracements, 128
sideways price movements, 79
signals, placement of orders, 123
significant locations, 28
software, TradeStation, 11
soybean futures, 130, 185
  1940-1941 trades
    examples, 140-143
    re-creation of, 144-150
  charts, 76, 148-149
S&P 500 Cash Index, 46
Stock Market Course, 4
stocks
  charts, 28
  plotting, 161
  Union Pacific, 2
  United States Steel, 2

stop loss orders, 123, 128. *See also*
  orders
  placement of, 123
  two-bar rules, 131
strengths, calculating, 33
styles, writing, 162-167
Sugar futures, 104
support, 31, 38, 108

T

T (time), 41. *See also* time
target prices, 33
Technical Analysis of the
  Financial Markets, 95
testing
  failures, 111
  validity of trendlines, 95
three-section bear markets, 9
three-section bull markets, 10
tick, 125
Ticker and Investment Digest, 1
time, 20-26
  50% retracements, 87
  calculations, 87
  double bottoms/tops, 57
  exceeding moves in, 41
tools, forecasting, 5. *See also*
  forecasting
tops
  buy old, 69-74
  double, 57-62
  triple, 49-54
tracking relationships, 26
TradeStation, 11
trading, 155
  charts, 155-160
  examples (1940-1941 soybean
    trades), 140-150

managing, 79, 119, 127-135
   exiting, 135-136
   placement of orders, 123-126
   reviewing, 136-138
   risk assessment, 120-122
   trade initiations, 126
markets, 39
   analysis, 12
   buy old tops/sell old
     bottoms, 69-74
   double bottoms/tops, 57-62
   exceeding moves in price,
     63-68
   exceeding moves in time, 41
   ranges, 80-83
   rapid moves, 74-80
   retracements, 86-93
   studying past, 155
   triple bottoms/tops, 49-54
methodologies, 5
phases, 39, 119
rules, 6-7
trailing stops, 135. *See also* stop
  loss orders
Transocean, Ltd., 51
trendlines, 95-103
trends, 9
  assessment, 39
  eighths retracement levels, 31
  profits, 40
  risk assessment, 122
triple bottoms/tops, 49-54
Truth of the Stock Tape, 4, 163
Tunnel Thru the Air, 4
two-bar rules, 130
  stop loss orders, 131
two-bar windows, 111
types
  of securities, 161
  of sideways price movements, 79
  of trendlines, 96

U

Union Pacific stock, 2
United States Steel stock, 2
up trendlines, 95-96
uptrends, 33, 80, 114. *See also*
  trends

V

validity of trendlines, testing, 95
values, Gold Chart Index, 114
vibration, 156
view of price movement, 27-31
volatility, 114

W

Wall Street Stock Selector, 4
weekly price actions, 63
wheat, commodity futures, 2
Williams %R, 106-108
windows, two-bar, 111
writing styles, 162-167
Wyckoff, Richard D., 1

X

x-axis, 87

Y

y-axis, 87

Z

zone consolidation, 100

FT Press

FINANCIAL TIMES

In an increasingly competitive world, it is quality
of thinking that gives an edge—an idea that opens new
doors, a technique that solves a problem, or an insight
that simply helps make sense of it all.

We work with leading authors in the various arenas
of business and finance to bring cutting-edge thinking
and best-learning practices to a global market.

It is our goal to create world-class print publications
and electronic products that give readers
knowledge and understanding that can then be
applied, whether studying or at work.

To find out more about our business
products, you can visit us at www.ftpress.com.